Professional
Excellence

Professional Excellence
Beyond Technical Competence

.

Alan Rossiter

AIChE₁₀₀

WILEY

A JOHN WILEY & SONS, INC., PUBLICATION

Library of Congress Cataloging-in-Publication Data is available.

ISBN 978-0-470-37737-6

Printed in the United States of America.

10 9 8 7 6 5 4 3 2 1

Dedication

To my teachers
To my students
To my professional colleagues
And most of all, to my family

Contents

Foreword

Work is important. Excellence in our work demands more than mere technical competence and conscientiousness in how we spend our time from 9 to 5. Its demands on all of us can become the heart and soul of our lives. In principle that is not a bad thing, but in real life hard work and commitment alone are not sufficient.

It is striking that one of the biggest factors driving support for the modern corporate social responsibility movement are the demands from the brightest young people—the people companies most want to recruit. Many young people today feel strongly about poverty and disadvantage, about the environment and climate change. Many want to be contributing to the solutions while they are at work, and not just in their time off work. Unlike a generation ago, they are not prepared to separate how they earn a living from what they believe in and value—and we should applaud them. Companies have to show potential recruits that they can meet this demand because, if they don't, the brightest young people will go off and work for companies that can commit to humanistic needs.

The dilemma between *what we do* and *who we are* is a recurring theme. The *Wall Street Journal* summed it up: "There is no right and wrong way to integrate work and family. There are only more or less costly ways in terms of career, relationships and health."

This dilemma is what *Professional Excellence* aims to reconcile. Down to earth advice on communication, relationships, celebration, and life/work balance are just some of the skills and issues explored.

Alan and I were student contemporaries, serving together in our Christian Union in what was for both of us a formative time. Based on his career as a chemical engineer, he unpacks a range of characteristics as well as the professional contexts within which they are used. Insights from management gurus provide academic credibility, while his personal experience provides a reality test from everyday professional life.

The book is deliberately nontechnical and practical, with anecdotes that help us stop, think, and reflect—activities that are all too rare in our busy "one-minute manager" world. Questions to aid reflection, whether on a long business trip or at a team meeting, are provided after each section.

There is humility too. The characteristics of excellence are not prescribed but suggested, not to be rigidly adopted but to be sensitively applied. Yet the wisdom is not mere pragmatism. It is based on values and ethical frameworks that this book helps us explore.

The final chapter captures for me the essence of this book. Alan's own health crisis illuminates for him—and for us readers— what is really important in life. People and relationships are our most valuable assets. I warmly commend this book.

RT HON STEPHEN TIMMS MP

Minister of State for Employment and Welfare Reform
Department for Work and Pensions, London SW1

Preface

I shouldn't have written this book. I am an engineer, not a leadership guru or a management consultant—much less a philosopher, psychologist, or ethicist. Yet after working as an engineer in industry for fifteen years, I felt that I had learned a bit about what was really important in the workplace, and I felt compelled to share it. Thus the original "In Search of Professional Excellence" article was born—and, to my surprise, it was published in *Chemical Engineering Progress*. That was in 1995, and almost immediately I received a request from a management journal to re-publish it. About the same time a professor asked if he could use the material in one of his courses, and shortly after that I started finding references to the article and extracts from it scattered around the Internet. Apparently there was some interest in what I had to say.

I wasn't able to develop the *Professional Excellence* material further until an opportunity arose in 2004 to run seminars and write a short course. This led eventually to the writing of this book. Stated simply, the book addresses the question "What, apart from your technical competence, is important in your career?" It considerably expands the original article, and incorporates material from various sources to complement my own anecdotes and observations. I have tried to make this book as practical as possible, with tools and tips to help professionals become more effective in their work, while also balancing their lives. The style is deliberately simple, with the objective of providing an "easy read" for time-pressured professionals and business people. I have also included questions after each chapter. These can be used for personal reflection or group discussion, to help readers assimilate and process the material.

Whether you are a seasoned practitioner or a newcomer to the world of work, I hope that you will enjoy this book and find in it some ideas that will challenge you and some tools that will help you as you to expand your own professional excellence.

ALAN ROSSITER

Bellaire, Texas
July 2008

Prologue: Posing a Question

It was after midnight as I left the airport at Portland, Maine. It was only fourteen hours since the flight arrangements had been made. When I called my wife (who was on maternity leave with our second child at the time) she had been philosophical about it. After all, this was fairly normal for our household. Since then I had missed one flight, been delayed on two others, changed airlines, and switched car rental companies. All in a day's work. The drizzle on the windshield obscured my vision as I set off into the December night—thankful that it was only drizzle, not snow. I headed toward I-95, and braced myself mentally for the two-hour drive to Rockland. As I did, I couldn't help asking the question, "Why am I doing this? Not just this particular crazy midnight adventure, but the whole deal. The inconvenience, the disruption to my personal life and my family—not to mention the sheer mental and physical demands. There are easier ways to make a living!" The drive ahead gave me a chance to ponder the question.

The company I worked for offered consulting services in a particular branch of engineering. It is rather specialized work—not the kind of thing that makes you a household name, though we did have a certain reputation among the aficionados of the process industries. As a result I got to travel around the world to study a wide variety of production facilities, ranging from oil refineries and petrochemical complexes to paper mills and food factories, and to recommend improvements. I still do similar work, but now as an independent consultant. But why do I do it? The drizzle turned to rain as I reached Route 1, and I started a mental list of possible reasons for my apparent insanity:

First, the work offers enormous variety. The technical challenges are wonderfully stimulating.

Second, although there is a great deal of satisfaction in solving challenging technical problems, it is better still when you can see that your solutions make a real difference to the people you are serving. From time to time I have that added pleasure.

Third, there is the professional camaraderie, and the mutual respect that has developed between myself and so many of the people with whom I have worked around the world.

Fourth, there is the "inertia factor." I have become quite well established in the overall field in which I work. It has taken years to reach this point. No doubt it would take years more if I wished to establish a similar position in another field. Much easier to stay where I am!

Fifth, I have had the opportunity to travel to places I scarcely dreamed I would ever see—Europe, China, Japan, South America, all over the United States and Canada—and also back to the place of my birth in Africa—all at other peoples' expense. True, the time for sightseeing has been rather limited, but the opportunities have been there, and I have taken them when I could.

Sixth, I meet so many fascinating individuals. Each project brings a new group of people into my life. The most obvious group, of course, consists of the professional peers who challenge and stimulate creativity. However, there are others that I encounter in the day-to-day process of living—the support staff, the families of professional colleagues, others that I meet socially around the world. All of them add color to my life.

Finally—although I would never have admitted this to my boss at the time—the pay isn't too bad.

The rain continued unabated as I drove through the streets of Rockland. As I approached the hotel, I tried to bring my meditations to a clear and concise conclusion. Why do I accept the inconvenience and disruption of the career I have chosen? How do I account for my apparent insanity? How can I explain it? Quite simple: I enjoy it. I enjoy the challenges, the variety, the people and the places, and I sincerely hope that I bring enjoyment to the people that I meet through my work. If it weren't for the elements of enjoyment and fulfillment, no amount of money, status or power—or anything else that people traditionally hope to get through their work—could possibly justify this craziness.

Part I

The World of Work

… the supreme quality for a leader is unquestionably integrity. Without it, no real success is possible, no matter whether it is on a section gang, a football field, in an army, or in an office. If a man's associates find him guilty of being a phony, if they find that he lacks forthright integrity, he will fail. His teachings and his actions must square with each other. The first great need, therefore, is integrity and high purpose.
—President Dwight D. Eisenhower

There has been a great deal of study on why people work, and what they expect to get from it. In this first main section we will examine some of the findings, and we will start to explore how the world of work interacts with the rest of life. In the process we will consider not only what we want to get out of our work but also what we need to put into it if we intend to pursue professional excellence, and we will look at how principles of ethics affect our professional life. The consideration of these topics provides a necessary foundation for our consideration of the elements of professional excellence in Part II of this book.

Chapter *1*

Motivated to Work

Le travail éloigne de nous trois grands maux: l'ennui, le vice et le besoin.—
Work banishes those three great evils, boredom, vice and poverty.
—Voltaire, Candide

Keep interested in your own career, however humble; it is a real
possession in the changing fortunes of time.
—Max Ehrmann, Desiderata

I have often wondered what other people think about their work.
A number of years ago, about the time I first started exploring the
idea of professional excellence, I decided to carry out an informal
and very unscientific survey in an effort to find out. I was in South
Africa on an extended assignment. One evening, while sitting at
dinner in the beautiful Eastern Transvaal with a few of my colleagues, I asked the loaded question, "Why are you doing the job
you do?"

The initial response was nervous laughter. The team worked
under me—I guess they were afraid of what the boss might think.
Then one of the group—predictably the most extroverted and
vocal member—said a single word: "Money!!"

However, as the evening wore on and the atmosphere mellowed, we returned to the subject, and came to some more considered conclusions. True, we need money to keep food on the table for ourselves and our families, but once that is taken care of, it ceases to be the main motivation. We have a wide range of other needs to meet—social needs and personal needs—and our work environment addresses many of these needs. These observations in the Eastern Transvaal reminded me of the findings of Abraham Maslow.

MASLOW IN THE WORKPLACE

Maslow, one of the founders of humanistic psychology in the 1960s, is perhaps best known for his "hierarchy of needs".[1,2] This is based on Maslow's observation that the human is a "wanting animal," and our basic wants can be classified in five basic levels (see Figure 1).

The foundation of the hierarchy—Level 1—is our *physiological* needs. These relate to the physical necessities of life, such as food and drink, shelter and clothing. Without these life itself is at risk, and unless we can satisfy these most basic of needs, we are not able to give our attention to much else.

Level 2 in the hierarchy deals with *safety*. This goes beyond the absence of physical danger. It includes a more general longing for comfort and security, like an infant resting in a mother's arms—or a worker assured of a weekly paycheck.

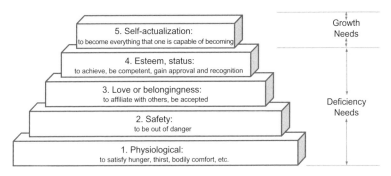

FIGURE 1   *Maslow's hierarchy of needs*

At Level 3 we find *love*. This includes the concept of romantic love, but its scope is much broader. It also encompasses the sense of belonging and being accepted. In the context of the workplace we see this in the camaraderie that develops among coworkers, and the sense of corporate identity and pride that people often share in business or project groups.

Level 4 addresses *esteem or status*. It is not enough simply to be accepted by our peers, to be "one of the group." People have an innate longing to be considered competent, to be admired, to be respected. Professional accolades, promotions, and awards can be a way of meeting this need. So can simple recognition of a job well done by peers, supervisors, and subordinates.

Level 5 in the hierarchy is *self-actualization*—that is, becoming everything that one is capable of becoming. We need more than just the respect of others. We need also to pursue our full potential. Once again, the workplace is an important part of this for many people. Professional development is an important vehicle that we can use to express our creativity, expand our capabilities, and grow as people.

In general, we fulfill the lower order "deficiency" needs first, and then our motivation shifts to the levels further up the hierarchy, ultimately toward the "growth needs" at the top level. However, this is not necessarily a rigid sequence. We can and often do function at multiple levels in the hierarchy simultaneously.

Providing for our survival needs and those of our families lies on the first and second levels of the hierarchy. We generally satisfy these needs with the material fruits of our labors, and this certainly provides one of the key motivations for work. However, we can fulfill these most basic objectives in any number of different ways, and the needs at Level 1 and Level 2 do not fully answer the question I asked in the Eastern Transvaal—how and why we choose our jobs. We need to look further to find a more complete solution to the puzzle.

Perhaps the most intriguing part of Maslow's hierarchy is Level 5, self-actualization, and this requires more explanation. Most earlier psychology researchers (notably Freud and his school) focused on clinical cases, and they drew their generalizations from these studies. Maslow observed that this necessarily resulted in a psychology of mental illness rather than mental health. By contrast, what Maslow set out to do was to study the scope of human potential, and to do so, he sought subjects who demonstrated the highest levels of attainment—"self-actualizing" people. His list of subjects included a number of historical figures, as well as public figures of his own time, among them Albert Einstein, Eleanor Roosevelt, and Albert Schweitzer. Based on his research (which included interviews where possible, as well as a study of public documents and historical records) he was able to determine characteristic drives or needs of these overachieving people, as summarized in Table 1.

TABLE 1   Characteristic Needs or Drives of Self-actualizing People

Truth	Individuality
Goodness	Perfection
Beauty	Order
Completion	Simplicity
Justice	Richness
Playfulness	Effortlessness
Self-sufficiency	Meaningfulness

Maslow noted that there was a measure of consistency between his findings and the views of certain classical Greek philosophers, notably Plato and Aristotle, who defined "the good life" in terms that are similar to the list in Table 1. Moreover Aristotle, like Maslow, had an interest in the full realization of human potential. He taught that this could be achieved, together with true happiness, through activities that are "consistent with the basic nature of humanity."[3]

There is also a significant overlap between Table 1 and virtues espoused within the Jewish and Christian traditions. Furthermore, and of great importance to our present discussion, many of the items in Table 1—Level 5 drives and needs—are major motivators in the workplace. We will examine this in more detail later.

JOB SATISFACTION

The conversation in the Eastern Transvaal continued between mouthfuls of South African beef and Mozambique prawns, and the subject shifted just a little. "So why are you in the specific job that you are doing now?" I asked.

With the more open atmosphere that now prevailed one of the quieter members of the group spoke out, summarizing his conclusions in a single word: "Satisfaction."

The conclusion my colleague reached echoes the wisdom of the ancients. King Solomon (ca. 900 BC) admonishes us: "A man can do nothing better than to eat and drink and find satisfaction in his work." (Ecclesiastes 2:24a) It also ties in with a great deal of contemporary research. For example, in a survey of chemical engineers in Britain and America[4] one respondent commented, "I'd work for free if I could afford to." Another stated, "Interesting, challenging work is what makes you get up in the morning." Money is still important, of course, and in the survey salary ranked third among the sources of job satisfaction, behind "interesting and challenging work" and "personal fulfillment." Human interactions also featured prominently, both positively and negatively, as key factors in job satisfaction. The top seven sources of satisfaction and dissatisfaction from the survey are summarized in Table 2.

More recent studies have identified similar findings. For example, *Time* magazine had a feature on the science of happiness in January 2005. This included an article on happiness in the workplace,[5] which referenced the following finding from a Gallup survey:

... [Gallup] says many companies are simply misreading what makes people happy at work. Beyond a certain minimum level, it isn't pay or benefits. It's strong relationships and a supportive boss.

TABLE 2   Top Seven Sources of Satisfaction and Dissatisfaction Reported by Engineers

Greatest Sources of Satisfaction	Greatest Sources of Dissatisfaction
1. Interesting and challenging work	1. Low career advancement potential
2. Personal fulfillment	2. Recognition from management
3. Salary	3. Job security
4. Autonomy on job	4. Financial resources
5. Job security	5. Salary
6. Career advancement potential	6. Work overload
7. Recognition from coworkers	7. Lack of support staff

It is also informative to see what can cause dissatisfaction or, worse, serious psychological problems in a professional working environment. All professions have characteristic difficulties. However, in reality the list of woes for teachers, social workers, and pastors is not too dissimilar to the problems encountered by doctors, scientists, engineers, and other professionals. Amy Stevens reports on a study that identified a wide range of factors as leading to severe depression, anxiety, insomnia, and related maladies among American lawyers.[6] These include:

- *Mismatch between personality and job requirements.* In particular, "introverted, thinking-type" people are often required to do "extroverted-type" things, like generating business.
- *Lack of feedback on work.* This problem is particularly acute for junior lawyers in large firms. They are often required to do a great deal of painstaking work for senior partners without any acknowledgment and without ever knowing the outcome of the labors. We need to know that we are significant, and that the work we do makes a difference.
- *Inability to separate self from work.* If we are too closely identified with the work we do we tend to take any work-related problem personally. This can be very damaging to self-esteem.
- *Poor public perception of lawyers, leading to negative self-image.* People tend to internalize the qualities projected on them by others. American society tends to portray lawyers as vicious sharks, and that can lead to deep internal conflicts for lawyers who really want to be "good boys and girls."
- *Conflicting demands placed on junior lawyers by senior lawyers.* The lines of authority in law firms tend not to be very clear. Often many senior partners make conflicting demands on a junior partner at one time, creating enormous stress.
- *Obsessional detail in the work.* Legal work can be detail-oriented and dull. This can cause severe frustration for those who practice it.

Next time you meet a lawyer, be nice to him or her. They have their problems, too!

However, work can also be a source of great satisfaction and fulfillment. It provides that satisfaction and fulfillment in a number of ways:

- *Attainment.* The sense of accomplishment that we have when we can look back at the end of a day, a week, a month, a year, a decade or a career, and review with pride the things that we have done.
- *Challenge.* The sense of adventure when we see daunting tasks before us and embrace them.
- *Recognition.* The sense of personal worth, which is a vital contributor to self-esteem. In part this comes from the salary we receive, but it also grows with the trust that people place in us day to day as we work.
- *Camaraderie.* The sense of belonging with the people with whom we work.
- *Security.* Not only because our work provides income but also because it can offer us a consistent and stable environment for many of our activities.
- *A creative outlet.* A way to express our imagination and abilities.

Work really does give us a reason for getting up in the morning. Many people decline rapidly after retiring, especially if they have no hobbies or outside interests to keep them busy. The explanation is simple: work—no matter how much we may complain about it—provides a major incentive for living.

Losing a job can be a devastating blow to self-esteem. As President Harry Truman put it, "It's a recession when your neighbor loses his job; it's a depression when you lose yours." The reasons for this reaction to losing a job go beyond the financial implications of joblessness. If you ask most working people the question: "What are you?" or "What do you do?" they will answer in terms of their job or profession: "I am a secretary, an engineer, a dentist," or "I work at a car factory, I mend household appliances, I drive a truck." Losing a job, therefore, can lead to a loss of personal identity, because in a very real sense my job is what I am. Arguably it should not be so, but for most of us it is.

Work can also be dangerous, for it can become all consuming, even addictive. For some, work can become a hiding place, a means of escaping from family or other responsibilities, or avoiding unpleasant issues that need to be addressed outside the workplace.

Even for those who do their best to balance the needs of career and family, work demands inevitably intrude into family life in potentially negative ways at certain times. Extended absences due to business "on the road" during critical stages of family development, conflicting needs in two-career households, or simply dealing with sick children while holding down a full-time job: These are the realities of life. A *Wall Street Journal* article a few years ago described several examples of families dealing with these types of problems.[7] It concludes with the following observation: "There is, many would say, no right or wrong way to integrate work and family. There are only more or less costly ways in terms of career, relationships, or health." We do well to pay attention to the problems and dangers, and to balance our career development with the other aspects of our lives. Sometimes we also have to make hard choices.

QUESTIONS FOR REFLECTION AND DISCUSSION

1.1. Compare Maslow's Hierarchy of Needs (Figure 1) and the top seven sources of satisfaction and dissatisfaction reported by engineers (Table 2). Complete the table below by matching each source of satisfaction and dissatisfaction against the most appropriate level in Maslow's hierarchy. (*Note*: Some items may fit in more than one level.)

MASLOW LEVEL	SOURCE OF SATISFACTION OR DISSATISFACTION
Level 1: Physiological	
Level 2: Safety	
Level 3: Love, belongingness	
Level 4: Esteem, status	
Level 5: Self-actualization	

At which level or levels do the largest number of items appear?

1.2. Do you agree with the need levels that Maslow proposes? Is it always necessary to satisfy the lower levels before proceeding to higher levels?

1.3. What are the greatest sources of satisfaction in your work?

1.4. What are the greatest sources of dissatisfaction in your work? What can you do to correct them?

Chapter 2

Life and Work

As you get older, you realize that philosophy and psychology are more important within a company than engineering.
—Troy Berg, a production manager for SSI Technologies in Janesville, Wis.

When I grow up I want to be a soccer player or the Easter Bunny.
—Daniel Rossiter, at age 3½.

During my university years my studies focused on mathematics and the physical sciences, and I vaguely assumed that this process was somehow preparing me for the "real world" beyond. It did not occur to me that perhaps there were other skills that could be equally important in my future career—indeed such thoughts seemed almost sacrilegious. Yet such I have found to be the case.

WHAT SKILLS DO YOU NEED?

A *Wall Street Journal* article in 1995 noted that engineering and other technical skills are essential in many companies, and excellence in these areas is at a premium.[8] The demand for technical skills in some areas is even more critical today. However, there is also a need for a wide range of "soft skills"—economics, marketing, personnel management, and especially communication—in today's technical people.

Significantly, most of the "soft skills" listed above are equally valuable outside the workplace—in the home and the community. Many people create an artificial separation between these roles: work and social life are somehow "different." This is a fallacy. Life is ultimately an integrated whole; there are inescapable links between the "professional me" and the "personal me." Two key thoughts help to explain why this is true:

- *All of life is about human relationships.* Other things are also important, of course, but in the final analysis it is only the way that we interact with one another that really counts.
- *All good human relationships are founded on the same principles.* That does not mean that the way we relate to, say, a three-year-old child is identical to the way we relate to the chairman of a Fortune 500 company, or to a spouse—although there are more similarities than one might think. The differences, however, are differences in application, not differences in principle.

The underlying principle of good relationships is constant: The key is consideration and respect for the other person. Most of us learned this principle in one form or another during our infancy. In Western culture its most common expression is the Golden Rule: "So in everything, do to others what you would have them do to you" (Matthew 7:12a); but it is striking that five hundred years before Jesus Christ, Confucius[9] taught the same principle in China.

Recent philosophers, ethicists, psychologists—and business people too—have also noted the validity of the principle, and some have proposed their own variants. One that I find intriguing comes from Houston icon Jim "Mattress Mac" McIngvale, owner of Gallery Furniture. He puts it this way: ". . . I find a sort of internal humor when I hear somebody suggest, 'Treat the customers like you would like to be treated!' That is patently incorrect! What we should be saying is, 'Treat customers like *they* want to be treated.' "[10] On a superficial reading McIngvale appears to contradict the Golden Rule. On closer inspection, however, he is really amplifying it. His point is that the "other person" (in this case, the customer) may not want to be treated the same way I do. I show greater respect (and, as a result, generate more business) by finding out how he or she really does want to be treated, and then treating him or her in that way.

Human interactions and behaviors can, of course, be incredibly complex, and it would be foolish to assume that all difficulties can be resolved instantly simply by applying this one rule. Nevertheless, this principle is extremely powerful and far-reaching, and we will see many other applications as we progress through this book.

The standard curriculum taught to engineers, scientists, lawyers, doctors, journalists, accountants, administrators, and most other professionals scarcely touches soft skills and principles of human interaction. They are considered more the realm of teachers, pastors, and mental health professionals. Academic training in technical disciplines tends to focus on the left-brain: logical, analytical thinking. The right brain, with its sensitive, intuitive, artistic focus tends to be neglected, even derided.

THE ROAD TO PROFESSIONAL EXCELLENCE

I passed through my years of formal education with surprisingly little thought about things of this nature, or more generally about the career that I would subsequently enter. It was easy to move through the system; after each academic year there was another, higher scholastic level to enter. Even at the end of my university days there wasn't much need for any profound thought about my future. I had a degree in chemical engineering from a good university, at a time when the job market for chemical engineers was buoyant. There was a natural progression into an entry-level chemical engineering position in a major company, and with this move I entered a whole new learning process—one that still goes on today, and will probably continue for the rest of my life.

The learning process has often seemed haphazard. Certainly it has not had much formal structure as almost all of it has been on the job, in the firing line; very little has been in classrooms. Yet these learning experiences are very important steps on the road to professional excellence.

What is professional excellence? How should we define "success" in our careers? Is it simply a matter of obtaining recognition for our work? Climbing the corporate ladder? Owning our own company? I think not. These are noble goals, of course, and may be a legitimate part of professional excellence for some people, but I believe we have to look for a wider definition.

Becoming proficient technically in our chosen field is probably the most obvious, and the least controversial, aspect of professional excellence. Few would argue against the importance of delivering accurate, technically correct work, and to do so consistently. During the course of our formal education we spend a great deal of time and effort learning the fundamentals of our chosen discipline. The principles and skills that we learn then are extremely valuable, and they form the foundation for the technical aspects of the work we do in our later lives. Once we enter the job market, we have opportunities to develop those skills further through practical experience, by interaction with professional colleagues, and at times, by specific training or research. This way we develop our most basic professional competence. However, although this is extremely important, it falls short of an adequate definition of professional excellence.

The skills required for true professional excellence must cover not just our basic technical competence but also the other disciplines that make us effective and productive in our careers. This includes soft skills such as communication, work management, interpersonal relationships, and balancing the conflicting demands that lay claim to our time and energies.

However, we cannot ultimately define professional excellence as list of skills. The individual skills are simply tools that we use to extend ourselves and expand our potential.

Professional excellence is the integration of all of the above factors to yield a balanced, productive and fulfilled individual who contributes positively in the workplace, the home, and in the wider community. It is not a final condition, but rather a growth process. Those who practice professional excellence are constantly striving to achieve these objectives by developing and applying the necessary skills, and by constructive interaction with others. This is an ongoing journey, a quest.

This definition does not preclude some of the more common concepts of success in relation to money and status—indeed those who practice professional excellence are very likely to do well in these areas too. However, the definition does preclude a narrow focus on "success" at any cost, and demands that due attention be given to the way in which we affect those around us by our actions and choices. The following quote from Ralph Waldo Emerson is one of the best expressions of this thought that I have seen:

> To laugh often and much; to win the respect of intelligent people and affection of children; to earn the appreciation of honest critics and endure the betrayal of false friends; to appreciate beauty, to find the best in others; to leave the world a bit better, whether by a healthy child, a garden patch or a redeemed social condition; to know even one life has breathed easier because you have lived. This is to have succeeded.

And, I would add, this is to have demonstrated professional excellence.

QUESTIONS FOR REFLECTION AND DISCUSSION

2.1a. If you are in full-time employment: What attracted you to your college major or your current career? When you started working, did you find that the content of the work matched your expectations?

2.1b. If you are a full-time student: Think about any experience you have in paid work or volunteer work. What skills were required in that work? To what extent has your formal schooling helped you to develop those skills?

2.2. How important are "soft skills" or "people skills" in your own job? What specific skills are needed? Do you make proportionate efforts to refine those skills? How?

2.3. Do you agree that the underlying principle for good interpersonal relationships is "consideration and respect for the other person"? Is this a principle that you were taught as part of your upbringing?

2.4. Do you feel that it is right to include positive contributions not only in the workplace but also in the home and in the wider community, within the definition of professional excellence? Why or why not?

Chapter 3

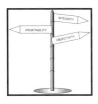

Ethics at Work

It horrifies me that ethics is only an optional extra at Harvard Business School.
— **Sir John Harvey-Jones, MBE**

Man is not a solitary animal, and so long as social life survives, self-realization cannot be the supreme principle of ethics.
— **Bertrand Russell**

The recognition that professional excellence integrates technical proficiency with interpersonal skills leads naturally to a consideration of ethics. Ethics, after all, deals with appropriate and inappropriate ways of treating people. This is a huge subject, but our scope in this chapter is restricted to an overview of systems of professional ethics—their form, applications, and limitations.

WHAT DO WE MEAN BY "ETHICS"?

Merriam-Webster's Dictionary[11] offers the following definitions for the word "ethics": "*1.* a discipline dealing with good and evil and with moral duty. *2.* moral principles or practice."

Professional Excellence: Beyond Technical Competence, by Alan Rossiter
Copyright © 2008 John Wiley & Sons, Inc.

In studying ethics, then, we are exploring good and evil, right and wrong. We are making value judgments and defining principles of conduct. We are deciding how we will behave, and how we will interact with other people.

Depending on which ethical system we adopt, different authorities may be invoked to define good conduct. We noted earlier that Aristotle taught that human potential could be fully realized through activities that are "consistent with the basic nature of humanity." In his system of ethics "good" is defined as "conforming to the pattern of nature." There are two other sources of authority that are commonly invoked in different ethical systems:

- The will of a deity, where good is defined as obedience to divine commands.
- The rule of reason, where behavior is expected to spring from rational thought.[12]

Modern Western ethical thinking incorporates elements from ethical systems, both sacred and secular, that invoke all of the authorities described above. The Greeks left an important legacy, and they provided much of the framework for modern systems of philosophy and ethics. This has a much more significant influence on modern life than most people realize. Jewish and Christian theology and philosophy have also been major factors in the development of Western thought, and continue to have a large impact on ethical standards. There are also many other influences, including existentialism (emphasizing the uniqueness of the individual) and numerous Eastern philosophical and religious systems. This complex mixture of ethical systems and perspectives has important implications in defining acceptable professional conduct, as we will see later in this chapter.

One area where there is a great deal of confusion is the distinction between ethics and law. The clear difference is the authority that is invoked. As we have seen, ethical systems invoke nature, rationality, or divine command as their authority. Laws invoke human authorities—usually a monarch or a governmental body—and each law is backed by sanctions imposed by human authorities. As we will see later, some codes of ethics are also incorporated into laws.

THE NEED FOR A CONSISTENT ETHICAL FRAMEWORK

Each of us tends to approach ethical choices based on our own particular ethical framework. To the extent that our framework is consistent with that of the people around us, it offers two important things to men and women of goodwill:

- An objective personal standard of action for those who subscribe to it.
- A common basis for evaluating the actions of others.

On the issue of a personal standard of action, consider the following two statements from popular literature:

> There is no good and evil, only power, and those too weak to seek it.
> —J. K. Rowling, *Harry Potter and the Sorcerer's Stone*

> With great power comes great responsibility.
> —Stan Lee and Steve Ditko, *Spider-Man*

Both of these statements deal with the use of power, although they come from very different perspectives. The speaker in the first statement (one of the villains who opposed Harry Potter) sees power as something to be sought above all else, and to be used for his own ends. In the second statement, Peter Parker's uncle Ben appeals to his nephew to recognize the power he has been given as a trust, something to be used responsibly and for the benefit of others.

I often present these two statements in seminars, and ask the audience to respond to them. Which one is more consistent with your own feelings and upbringing? Of course, most people say they agree with the sentiment of the Spider-Man quote. The Harry Potter quote, after all, comes from a villain. However, while this is true, the reality is that there are people in our world who do abuse power, and if we are totally honest, we are all capable of doing the same, given the opportunity.

What prevents us from doing this? If we have a framework of ethics that addresses the use of power—or any other aspect of our personal or professional conduct—we can use it as the standard for our own actions, and thus avoid inappropriate behaviors.

Professional societies, businesses, and other organizations often codify their ethical frameworks, as we will discuss in more detail later in this chapter. This provides a common point of reference for all members within any such body to use in deciding ethical matters. Many of these bodies apply sanctions against members who violate their codes, and there may also be legal consequences for noncompliance. These potentially negative outcomes can be a powerful motivator to comply. However, this is not really a sufficient basis for producing ethical behavior—a subject to which we will return shortly.

Let's now turn to the matter of having a common basis for evaluating the actions of others. As we have seen, people within Western society today represent a great variety of philosophical and ethical viewpoints, and these viewpoints often contradict one another in significant ways. This point was brought home to me forcefully a few months ago when an engineering student from the Far East visited my home. Looking over my bookshelf, he commented that he had seen one of the books in his own country but that the cover looked different. On further discussion he told me that in his homeland it was common practice to take books to a copy shop, where a complete bound copy would be made. In the United States or Europe, of course, this type of thing would not happen (not openly, at least) because of our intellectual property laws. However, such concerns apparently do not arise in his country. What made this incident particularly striking to me was the fact that I was the author of the book he had noticed. It was my royalties that were not being paid!

Could I reasonably judge my young friend for his lax attitude toward intellectual property rights? Probably not. His culture did not provide him with the same ethical framework in this area as mine did. However, while he was in the United States he was naturally bound by US laws, and could not simply copy entire books at the local copy shop (a legal issue). An ethical framework that recognized the concept of intellectual property would place the same responsibility upon him, whether or not he was in the United States and subject to US legal sanctions (an ethical issue). If he and I both subscribed to the same ethical framework, and he chose to violate these rights, then I would have a reasonable basis for contesting his actions, whether or not he was in a country whose laws allowed him to act in this way.

PHILOSOPHIES OF SERVICE

We have seen that an ethical framework can guide our choices. However, we have also noted that there are many different influences in the ethical arena, and we therefore cannot assume that everyone is using the same framework to form judgments and make choices. This makes it important to agree and to document the basis on which ethical issues are to be decided. In the context of professional activities, this is often accomplished by developing a concise statement of philosophy.

One of the oldest and best-known statements of professional philosophy and ethics is the Hippocratic Oath (see text in Appendix 1), which is generally ascribed to Hippocrates of Cos (460–370 BC) or to one of his students. The Oath defines the obligations of the medical profession, although it is now mostly of historical and traditional value.

The Hippocratic Oath addresses the key issues in medical ethics, the most important being a sense of responsibility to a patient. The ideal physician should keep himself or herself and the profession "holy and upright." Furthermore the Oath assures patients of professional confidentiality.

The Hippocratic Oath is not strictly a code of professional ethics. Rather, as its name implies, it is an oath—a solemn promise and commitment. Many other professional bodies have adopted similar statements of their responsibilities and professional obligations. For example, in June 1954 the National Society of Professional Engineers (NSPE) in the United States approved "The Engineers' Creed" as a statement of philosophy of service for engineers[13]:

> As a Professional Engineer, I dedicate my professional knowledge and skill to the advancement and betterment of human welfare.
>
> I pledge:
>
> To give the utmost of performance;

To participate in none but honest enterprise;

To live and work according to the laws of man and the highest standards of professional conduct;

To place service before profit, the honor and standing of the profession before personal advantage, and the public welfare above all other considerations.

In humility and with need for Divine Guidance, I make this pledge.

(Reprinted by Permission of the National Society of Professional Engineers)

The Engineers' Creed is similar to the Hippocratic Oath in emphasizing truthfulness, faithfulness, honor, and integrity as priorities for the individual practitioner, and the need to maintain the standing of the profession itself. The main distinctive feature of the NSPE code, which is shared with other statements of engineering ethics, is its emphasis on public welfare, which is a central theme of engineering work and responsibility.

CODES OF PROFESSIONAL ETHICS

Most professional organizations have a code of ethics that their members are required to uphold. Codes of this type expand the concept of a statement of philosophy into an organized system that defines the ethical framework that members of the profession are expected to use, and details how this is to be applied in specific situations. In some cases the code of ethics is provided simply as guidance for the organization's membership, but in other cases, especially where professional licensing bodies are involved, this is backed up by law and supported by specified disciplinary actions in the event of noncompliance. Many corporations also have their own codes of ethics.

Among the engineering disciplines, the various engineering institutions (chemical, mechanical, civil, structural, etc.) each have their own code of ethics. However, in the United States the most frequently cited code of engineering ethics is the one adopted by the National Society of Professional Engineers,[14] as this is designed to address the needs of all engineering disciplines. This code builds on the concepts introduced in the Engineers' Creed and provides specific applications in a wide range of areas. The various sections in the code explain how engineers are required to:

1. Hold paramount the safety, health and welfare of the public.
2. Perform services only in areas of their competence.
3. Issue public statements only in an objective and truthful manner.
4. Act for each employer or client as faithful agents or trustees.
5. Avoid deceptive acts.
6. Conduct themselves honorably, responsibly, ethically, and lawfully so as to enhance the honor, reputation, and usefulness of the profession.

Codes of ethics have an important part to play in establishing appropriate conduct in business and professional life. However, there are limitations to what they can accomplish. There is no guarantee that we will follow the requirements of any code of ethics simply because we are familiar with its requirements. The reality is that our conduct is the product of what we think—our beliefs, attitudes, and opinions—our personal value system.

Much of our value system is internalized during our early years—before we even know (much less care) about the existence of codes of ethics. If our internal value system is consistent with the requirements of a specific ethical code, it will be natural to follow the requirements of that code and to look to the code to help in resolving difficult issues. However, if the requirements of the code are inconsistent with our established internal value system, it will be much more difficult to comply.

It is also important to be aware that codes of ethics—and even statements of professional philosophy—can and do change over time. This is true even though the basic principles of human interaction themselves are timeless. Technology is constantly advancing, and society itself is also changing. Ethical constructs are modified and adapted in response.

In 1973 the US Supreme Court rejected the Hippocratic Oath as a guide to medical ethics and practice.[15] The Justices ruled that the Oath is no longer capable of covering the latest developments and methods of medical practice and research. The NSPE code also has been through several revisions in recent years, and so have the codes of ethics for other professional bodies.

QUESTIONS FOR REFLECTION AND DISCUSSION

3.1. The author lists three different sources of authority that are invoked in ethical systems: the will of a deity, the pattern of nature, and the rule of reason. How do you view these different authorities? Which source of authority do you seek to follow when making ethical choices?

3.2. What are the benefits of having a code of professional ethics? How does the cultural diversity of our society affect your answer?

3.3. The chapter ends by noting that codes of ethics change over time, in response to advances in technology and changes in society. In your opinion, does this lessen or increase the value of codes of ethics?

Part II

Elements of Professional Excellence

"Business!" cried the Ghost, wringing its hands again. "Mankind was my business. The common welfare was my business; charity, mercy, forbearance, and benevolence, were, all, my business. The dealings of my trade were but a drop of water in the comprehensive ocean of my business!"
—**Charles Dickens, A Christmas Carol**

In Part I we noted that professional excellence is much more than technical proficiency. At a technical level, most work is about things: building them, selling them, moving them, improving them. It is about projects with tangible, physical results. Life, however, is about interacting with people. It is about relationships. Professional excellence blends these two dimensions of "things" and "people."

We need technically competent professionals in all disciplines. Indeed we cannot function in modern society without them. Yet beyond technical competence we need people who create an atmosphere of trust and goodwill. We work far better with and for people we like and trust than people we merely respect or fear.

So where should we focus in order to increase our professional excellence? The list below itemizes seven key elements or characteristics that we need to develop:

1. Communicating effectively
2. Fulfilling commitments
3. Recognizing and expanding your professional limits
4. Investing in your profession and in your community
5. Affirming your coworkers
6. Celebrating your work
7. Protecting your personal life

These elements are discussed in the chapters that follow.

Chapter 4

Communicating Effectively

It's not the writing that's difficult—it's the thinking
—James Leigh

You can have brilliant ideas, but if you can't get them across, your ideas won't get you anywhere.
—Lee Iacocca

The genius of communication is the ability to be both totally honest and totally kind at the same time.
—John Powell

Communication—written and verbal—is fundamental to business and to all of life, and it underpins all of the elements of professional excellence to a greater or lesser extent. However many professionals—especially those whose training and is scientific or technical—struggle to communicate effectively.

In this chapter we explore some of the reasons for and barriers to effective communication, and provide some guidelines and techniques to improve communication. The chapter starts with general principles, and then introduces specific skills. It ends with a brief discussion of miscommunication.

REASONS AND BARRIERS

Consider the Purpose of Your Communication

Why do we communicate? The question seems trite, but it is evident from much of the miscommunication that occurs that the answer is not as obvious as it may appear.

There are two main reasons for communication: conveying information, and soliciting responses. However, of the two the latter is really the more fundamental, for we rarely disseminate information just for the fun of it. When we give out information, we are almost always looking for a response. The response we are seeking may be an order from a client, a raise from the boss, sympathy from a friend, a laugh, an attitude adjustment in a rebellious child, a compliment—or anything in between. Yet often we are so engrossed in our own inner world that we forget our objective and communicate totally inappropriately. As a father I have often been caught out in exactly that way—responding sharply to correct misbehavior, and forgetting that this is exactly what an attention-seeking four-year-old wants.

Much work that contains a great deal of technical value gets ignored because the people who did the work failed to communicate properly. While we are engrossed in a fascinating project, it is very easy to forget that the rest of the world is largely ignorant of what we are doing. We tend to assume that our management, our customers, and the world in general will be as knowledgeable as we are. We therefore tend to communicate at an "expert" level.

All communication, then, should be structured with its objective in mind. It should also be targeted at its intended audience. When I was a young engineer at ICI, it was a standing joke that anything written for managers should be in words of one syllable. Many years later I respect the wisdom behind the joke. It is not that all managers are inherently stupid. Managers often have to make judgments in areas outside their own expertise, and they need clear, concise guidance to help them make those judgments. Those called upon to help them need to keep this in mind when presenting their reports.

There are instances, of course, where "expert" reports and papers are appropriate—but these are generally in "expert forums" where the listener or reader shares the appropriate background. For nonexpert audiences (by far the majority) this approach is wholly inappropriate. The key point is that professional excellence includes a commitment to communication that informs selected audiences and evokes intended responses, rather than simply presenting the things that fascinate us individually.

This principle can be extended. It is not just when we prepare reports that we need to consider the needs of our audiences and how they will respond to what we say or write—it is true at every stage of our work, and in every part of our lives.

Remember to Listen as Well as Speak

One of the joys of fatherhood is the opportunity it gives for revisiting the things of childhood. My two boys love books, and when they were young, I often got to read to them. It is amazing how much more I see in children's literature now than ever I did as a child. Consider, for example, the wisdom of the nursery rhyme "A Wise Old Owl":

> A wise old owl lived in an oak;
>
> The more he saw the less he spoke;
>
> The less he talked the more he heard;
>
> Shouldn't we be like that wise old bird?

The wisdom of that old bird is applicable to adults at least as much as it is to children. Communication is a two-way street. It is about obtaining desired responses in our audience. Given this premise, it is clear that we must hear and understand our listeners, recognize their needs and desires, be sensitive to their "hot buttons," put ourselves in their shoes—for only then can we anticipate their responses. Stephen Covey[16] expresses this idea in the exhortation,

"Seek to understand—then to be understood." I have found this to be a valuable principle, but also a remarkably difficult thing to do in practice.

Why is it so hard? The reason lies deep in the ego. All of us want have our opinions heard. If I have put a lot of work into a project, I want to be able talk about what I did and the results I obtained. If someone has offended me in some way, I feel that I have a right to talk about it and get sympathy and support. And even if I don't have anything consequential to say right now, I still want to be noticed, to feel that I am significant. These are very natural reactions, but they are serious barriers to effective communication. They reverse the order: They put my need to be understood ahead of my need to understand you.

Overcoming this barrier to communication requires discipline. We must determine to listen and to understand what the other person is trying to tell us. When the urge comes to interrupt and say our piece, we need to master that urge. One technique that is often effective is to write down the thing you want to say, and then wait until an appropriate point arises in the conversation to say it without disrupting others. By writing something down, we assure ourselves that we won't forget the point we want to make, and that relieves a large part of the stress of the situation.

Practice Both Types of Listening

There are two types of information that people generally convey—factual and emotional. We need to be constantly listening for both of these types of information.

Consider a simple statement such as "It is ten pm." The factual content is very simple: it is just a statement about the time of day. However, the emotional content can vary enormously depending on circumstances. If the speaker is someone whose favorite TV program starts at ten, it might convey eager anticipation. If the speaker normally goes to bed early, it might convey fatigue. If the speaker is a parent greeting an arriving teenager who was supposed to get home at nine o'clock . . . you get the idea.

Listening for factual content is a logical function—that is, we are identifying the plain, surface meaning of the words we hear. For most of us—especially those who are technically trained—this is by far the easier type of listening. Nevertheless, people often get it wrong, largely because they are preoccupied. For example, it is very common that a question is asked and the answer that is given does not address the issue at all. This often happens in casual conversations. I have also, however, observed the same phenomenon in technical presentations and business discussions. If we are to overcome this problem, we must exercise the discipline of listening and understanding. When in doubt, ask the questioner to repeat or rephrase the question.

Listening for emotional content is an altogether tougher assignment for most of us. We all accept the reality of emotion in communication, and the example above of the teenager's late return home at ten o'clock illustrates this. Yet the fact is that most of us are not trained to recognize emotional messages, much less to respond to them. However, until we deal with the emotions that arise we are unlikely to be able to convey our own message effectively.

How should we handle the emotions—especially the negative ones—that are conveyed to us? The following three basic principles can be extremely helpful:

- Acknowledge the reality of the emotions
- Take them seriously
- Be accepting and nonjudgmental

These principles are remarkably versatile. They apply equally to the home and the workplace, to anguished three-year-olds and rugged fifty-year-olds. A recent experience illustrated their application in the workplace very powerfully:

I had made some recommendations that would involve adding some equipment in a client's plant. A meeting was called to discuss the idea with the technical and operating staff that would be involved in the project. The meeting seemed to be going well until the maintenance superintendent turned to me and demanded: "How am I going to maintain the new equipment?" The question was clearly charged with emotion. I did not realize this at the time, but there had been manpower cuts, and the maintenance department was struggling to meet the demands that were being made on it. However,

I recognized the exasperation in the superintendent's voice. The only comment that I could offer was a very simple but truthful one: "You have a good point. The new equipment will require maintenance." There was a brief silence. Then several people, including the superintendent, started offering suggestions on how to overcome the problem. By the end of the meeting the superintendent had calmed down, and although I can't claim he was enthusiastic, he did at least acknowledge that the project was workable. The key was that the rest of us had acknowledged the potential difficulty that he faced. To the superintendent, this was far more important than the possible solutions that we had offered.

Don't Speak Impulsively

Ill-considered words can be very destructive, professionally and personally. Once the words have been spoken, they cannot be taken back. Anger, frustration, and impatience are enemies of effective communication—and they can be very damaging to careers, to communities, and to families.

I am not a naturally calm person, and the closest I have come to getting fired was the direct result of impulsive speech. My organization was working in collaboration with a large foreign engineering firm on a process design for a large refinery. Prior to an important meeting with our client we sat down with our collaborators to discuss progress. Their lead engineer praised our work, and said they planned to modify their original design significantly based on our input. However, the next day, when we met with the client, the same lead engineer said that none of my organization's ideas were workable, and they would not be incorporated in the design. As he spoke I felt a growing sense of indignation, until I finally interjected, "Wait a minute! That's not what you said yesterday!"

The room fell silent for a long moment. Then the lead engineer from the client company, smiling, quietly said, "It seems that you need to get back together and decide what you really think."

To be fair on myself, the situation was complicated by differences in culture, and possibly also some language problems. However, whatever the extenuating circumstances could have been, that incident caused a severe strain between my organization and our collaborator for a long time.

That episode highlighted my need to control my temper and manage my impulsiveness. The lesson is simple: When in doubt, hold your tongue. This calls for a high level of restraint. But to the extent that you can achieve it, you can avoid a lot of grief both at work and in your private life.

PRINCIPLES FOR EFFECTIVE SPEAKING AND WRITING

There are many books and articles that deal with basic writing and verbal skills for business and professional people.[17–19] These provide a lot of helpful guidance on techniques for written and verbal presentations, and together with a good dictionary and a thesaurus they can greatly improve the quality of our communication. However, it is not my intention here to deal with the minutiae of grammar and style, important though these things are. Rather, my primary goal is to set out principles that underpin all effective communications. The skills required to communicate effectively are necessarily built on these principles.

Convey the Right Attitude, Not Just the Right the Information

As we have already seen, our objective in communication is to obtain desired responses in our audience. Communication is more than just delivering the factual content of a message. How we deliver it is equally important. There is a very simple formula:

- I like you—therefore I like what you say.
- I don't like you—therefore I don't like what you say.

What are the characteristics that promote a positive response from the audience—a favorable attitude to me personally, and an agreement to proceed in the desired direction? We can never hope to "click" with everyone. However, it is self-evident that confidence is an important factor. Few people will follow the lead of someone who plainly has no idea where he or she is going. Having said that, it is also clear that people will not respond favorably to arrogance and superior attitudes. Confidence must not give way to conceit and presumption. We all resent being disregarded, but appreciate it when we are acknowledged as significant and our opinions as important. The example of the maintenance superintendent in a previous section is a case in point. Once the importance of an individual's contribution has been recognized, he or she will often become an ally, and set out to overcome the problems involved in achieving jointly accepted goals. This approach doesn't always work, of course, but it is far superior to confrontation.

Don't Be Afraid to Ask for Advice

There are at least three benefits of asking someone for counsel: First, it puts me in my proper place—as someone who is still learning, and wants to learn more. Second, if the advice is good, it might help me to solve a problem. And third, it is likely to gain me a friend, or at least an ally.

A request for advice is one of the highest compliments that can be paid. It says implicitly that I respect the views of the person whose counsel I seek, and very few people resent being asked—occasionally—for this kind of assistance. Of course, the high esteem associated with being an advisor means that we should not bestow this honor arbitrarily. Don't ask people to advise you if you have no intention of following their advice.

The main idea here can best be summarized in this thought: Effective communication flows out of vulnerability. In order to be granted access into another person's world, I have to expose my own humanity, at least in some measure. Pseudo-infallibility is not a part of professional excellence.

Keep Things Simple

There is a temptation, as discussed earlier, to include a great deal of technical detail when in fact it is inappropriate to do so. We are not usually obliged to tell all. Indeed in most circumstances it is exceedingly improper to do so.

We need to practice the discipline of simplicity. Good communication involves identifying key ideas and highlighting them. Non-essentials can usually be discarded in verbal presentations, and relegated to appendixes in written reports.

My experience in making verbal presentations is that if they are not so simple that I feel embarrassed, then they are probably too complex. As I mentioned earlier in this chapter, we generally make presentations on subjects in which we are, to some degree at least, experts—even though we may not feel like it. Few audiences feel insulted if we help them with the basics.

If you are using visual aids, make sure they are clear and uncluttered. More than one central idea per slide will generally lead to confusion. If there are one or two people in the group who want to know more of the details, invite them to talk privately after the formal presentation.

Structure Your a Presentation Carefully

Karen Beck[20] recommends that the main body of a business presentation should have between three and five main points, with all of the information organized as subpoints under them. Limiting the number of main points makes the presentation much easier for the audience to follow, but the use of subpoints allows the presenter to include as much information as necessary in the presentation. In addition to the main body of the presentation, there needs also to be an introduction to establish rapport with the audience and to explain the purpose of the presentation, and a conclusion, to summarize the message of the presentation and to provide a call to action.

Structure Your Written Reports Too

It is particularly important to keep in mind that different parts of the report will generally be read by different groups of people. An executive summary, for example, is likely to go to far more people than the body of a report. Moreover many of its readers will know little of the detail of the work, and some of those readers may be senior executives. The executive summary is therefore the most important part of the report. It should be concise (usually no more than one page long), and should contain information only on key subjects of general interest—the objectives of the work, results, and recommendations. Other special features of the work (e.g., new methods used) may sometimes be included.

Only people who are more familiar with the work will usually read the main body of a report. They often have educational backgrounds and experience levels similar to those of the report's author, and can reasonably be expected to understand technical information. However, the structure of the report must be clear and uncluttered. Any details that are not central to the main message of the report belong in appendixes or footnotes. Remember the "KISS" principle: "Keep it Simple, Stupid!"

Start Writing Sooner Rather Than Later

Typically we write reports to document a piece of work—a research project, the results of some calculations, a survey, and so on. The tendency for many people is to do the writing when the rest of the work is complete. Generally, this is a bad idea. The writing is an integral part of the overall project, not just a "necessary evil" to be handled when the "real work" is complete.

It is usually very helpful to develop an outline of your report—the overall structure and also, if possible, the main topics—early in the work. This can serve as a framework and a guide for the project as a whole. The various tasks in the project are conducted to provide content for the different sections of the report.

As the work progresses, you can draft individual parts of the report. Very often this process highlights areas where information is missing, or suggests areas where you might like to do additional research or calculations. The result is not just a better report but a better, more complete, piece of technical work too.

Use Humor When Appropriate

Humor is a powerful communication tool. However, only rarely does it fit in formal written technical reports. The problem is that a joke stands in lonesome incongruity in the midst of an impersonal document whose readers may never have met the authors.

However, humor can have a useful role in limited circulation reports whose readers are all coworkers. It can also be used to good effect in instruction manuals—computer guides, for example. Documents of this type can be extremely dull and boring, but a little humor, properly used, can make them much more readable. One of the best ways to add humor in these situations is through simple graphics—for example, with clip art.

In contrast to the very limited role of humor in written reports, a good belly laugh is an essential component of any live presentation. It offers two important benefits:

- It raises the "energy level" of the audience, and can help to keep their attention.
- It humanizes the presenter. He or she is no longer just a reporter, but a fellow human being in the eyes of the audience, and is therefore more readily accepted.

Humor must not be overdone, however, or it will detract from the more serious message. For the same reason any jokes we tell in a presentation should be relevant to our message in some way, or they tend to block rather than aid our delivery.

MISCOMMUNICATION

Very often we think we have communicated effectively, but in practice the message has not been received correctly. This problem is illustrated by a story (probably untrue) that is told of a British commander in the trenches during the First World War. After sizing up his local situation, he decided it was time to move forward, so he told the soldier nearest him in the trench to pass this message along the line: "Send reinforcements, we're going to advance!" The soldier repeated this to the man next to him, and so on down the line until the message reached its intended recipient. However, by then the wording had changed to: "Send three and four pence, we're going to a dance!" What happened next is not reported, but it probably was not the most successful military action of the war.

Why Does Miscommunication Occur?

Sometimes, in the case of verbal communication, the problem is purely physical: the listener cannot hear what the speaker is saying. This was most likely the source of difficulty in the story above from the First World War trenches. However, when people really cannot hear what is said in business, professional, or family settings, they will usually ask the speaker to repeat the statement.

A very common, but potentially much more serious, type of miscommunication occurs when the hearer believes he has heard what the speaker has said, but in reality he has misinterpreted it. The usual reason for the misinterpretation is differences of perception, inclination, or need. Consider the following question: "Do you prefer Coke or Pepsi?" How might you understand the question? If you are thirsty, and you happen to like Pepsi, you might believe it to be an offer, in which case you would reply "Pepsi, please." On the other hand, especially if you have just had your fill of food and drink, and have no desire for any more at the present time, you would probably assume the question a simple request for information on your preferences in soft drinks. There again, if you are a keen investor, you might take it as a request for a stock market tip.

This is a rather trivial example (unless you happen to work for the Coca Cola Company or PepsiCo), but the principle has far-reaching implications in day-to-day communications. We cannot simply assume that because we know what we mean everyone else will also understand. Differences in background, language, or education, or differences in perspective, easily introduce misunderstandings. For example, the buyer and the seller in any transaction usually "hear" different things. If the seller says "the price is somewhere between $50 and $100," he probably means that it is $99.95, or thereabouts. The buyer almost certainly "hears" $50.

When others appear not to understand what we are trying to communicate we need to recognize that at least part of the fault lies with us. Communication is a two-part process, with a "transmitter" and a "receiver" involved. As far as possible we should establish the interests, backgrounds, and needs of the audience, and tailor the contents of the message accordingly. Wherever possible, we should state our assumptions about those interests, backgrounds, and needs. If the assumptions are wrong, it is better that everyone knows as soon as possible. If we are "transmitting" in a forum where feedback is possible, it is highly desirable to ask questions periodically—not just to make sure the audience is awake, but more important, to check that they understand what we are saying, and then make adjustments as needed.

Some Misunderstandings Are Inevitable

Misunderstandings happen both in our professional life and our personal life. How many people can honestly claim that they have never had misunderstandings with a friend or spouse? Misunderstandings are invariably the result of poor communication and/or incompatible assumptions (as in the drink choice example of the previous section).

In the professional context, one area where misunderstandings are rampant is at the supplier/customer interface. In this context the "supplier" and "customer" need not necessarily be in separate companies. They may simply be different departments of the same company, or even two individuals in the same group, one of whom is providing goods or services for the other.

In order to minimize this problem, it is important that both the supplier and the customer communicate clearly about their expectations before committing to an agreement. This often requires multiple iterations to resolve all the issues. After an agreement has been reached and work starts, it is a good idea to check periodically to make sure the project is on the right track too. On more than one occasion I have participated in assignments where the final deliverables bore little resemblance to the original proposal, because it became clear that the initial concept was inappropriate. Of course, we should not make changes in scope arbitrarily or unilaterally. All affected parties must understand and agree to the changes, and this includes any impact on cost and schedule.

When misunderstandings arise, it is essential to resolve them quickly and amicably; otherwise, they are likely to escalate. Many friendships, marriages, and professional relationships have been destroyed because of this.

Some Communication Is Designed to Deceive

The situations where I have seen deliberate miscommunications most often are in commercial negotiations and in job applications, although deliberate technical miscommunication can occur too. We deal with this topic in more detail in a later section, so for the moment all that I will say is this: Deliberate misunderstandings and misinformation seem to be "business as usual" with certain individuals and organizations. Such practices are tantamount to premeditated lies, whatever the motivation may be. They are unethical, and have no place among the ranks of the professionally excellent, where business and personal relationships are based on trust and mutual respect. The key principle is integrity—being who we are, and not pretending to be what we are not. But sometimes you have to swim with sharks, so be prepared.

QUESTIONS FOR REFLECTION AND DISCUSSION

4.1. The author states two main reasons for communicating: conveying information, and soliciting responses. Do you agree with this? Can you think of any other reasons that communication occurs?

4.2. Why is listening an important part of communication, and why is it difficult to do? How good are you at listening during conversations?

4.3. What two basic types of information does most communication convey? Are you better at identifying the emotional content of communication, or the factual component?

4.4. Why is it important to ensure that presentations and reports are well-organized? What are the main barriers to good organization?

4.5. Have you encountered examples of deliberate miscommunication? What were the results of the miscommunication? Give examples.

Chapter *5*

Fulfilling Commitments

The reason that most major goals are not achieved is that we spend our time doing second things first.
—Robert J. McKain

How does a project get to be a year behind schedule? One day at a time.
—Fred Brooks

Time is the most valuable thing a man can spend.
—Diogenes

Doing good technical work and communicating it well are both important, but they are not enough. Our ability to deliver on time is often critical. In business large capital commitments and major revenue streams are often dependent on our work, and the old adage about time being money could hardly be more appropriate.

Despite the acknowledged importance of the time factor, too often schedules are allowed to slip and deadlines are not met. This may reflect a lack of commitment either corporately or individually.

However, in most cases the real reasons lie in poor planning and organization. People don't set out to miss their targets. They simply sink in a quagmire of conflicting priorities and can't drag themselves out. The result is frustration and a sense of failure for the individuals concerned, compounded by the displeasure of supervisors and clients—not a happy situation for anyone.

How can we improve our performance in meeting schedules and fulfilling commitments in general? Over the years I have seen both successes and failures in this area, and I have been a part of both. Several common threads stand out from these experiences.

In this chapter we will look at some general principles that help us deliver on commitments, examine a powerful tool for prioritization, and explore some tips to improve our efficiency in time management.

GENERAL PRINCIPLES

Be Realistic

Overzealous selling and overanxious management often result in timeframes being set that cannot be achieved in practice. As professionals we all generally have some input into the planning of the work we do, and it is important that we use this to establish schedules that can realistically be met. This applies both to the work we do for "paying clients" and also to other professional activities such as publications, which also carry schedules and deadlines.

The ideal schedule is challenging but achievable. The "challenging" aspect is necessary for two reasons:

First, the "time is money" principle applies: the quicker jobs are done, the greater is the revenue that can be generated. Invoicing can be carried out more quickly, cash flow can be improved, and more work can be carried out in any given time period.

One situation where this principle appears to be violated is in "time and materials" or "reimbursable" contracts, where payment is based on time worked rather than on specific deliverables. There are situations where this approach makes sense—notably where the scope of work cannot be defined accurately before a job starts. Clearly, contracts of this type can encourage inefficient work practices, as there is no immediate incentive for the contractor to operate efficiently. However, any organization or individual that gains a reputation for billing excessive work-hours will lose business to more efficient competition in the long run, so the "time is money" principle still applies.

Second, "challenge" is what keeps us sharp in our work. If schedules are set with too much slack in them, it is easy for those doing the work to become complacent and bored. It is a fallacy that allowing more time necessarily results in a better—or even a more thorough—job. The time allocated to the work must be adequate but not excessive.

The key to setting an appropriate schedule is knowing your own work rate and that of any other people who will perform any of the required tasks. This is essentially a matter of experience. Some organizations have well-established time quotas for specific jobs—for example, garages often list the hours required for their mechanics to perform common repairs on cars. Where the work tends to consist of unique one-off jobs, estimation is more difficult and requires more ingenious methods if it is to be done accurately. Spreadsheets and scheduling software are increasingly providing powerful tools for assisting in this task. However, when projecting time requirements, there is no substitute for the experience of people who have done similar jobs before, and knowing the abilities of the people who will actually do the work.

One warning: I commented earlier that the time allocated to a task must be adequate but not excessive. In our attempts to minimize time on a job, it is very easy to overschedule. This is risky—you don't know what tomorrow may bring. Some slack is always desirable in any schedule because in our imperfect world there will always be some unexpected but legitimate demands to pull you or your organization away from the tasks that you planned to do. However, these demands must be mastered; they must not be allowed to master us. This concept is expanded later in the chapter.

Be Committed

Having agreed on a schedule, we must be committed, both personally and corporately, to fulfilling our agreement. Legitimate professionals do not agree to do things in a certain time if they don't plan to fulfill the agreement. This is an ethical issue. However, reality has a way of deflecting good intentions that are not backed up by genuine commitment.

At a personal level, there are always multitudes of things demanding our attention, and it is very easy to be deflected from our agreed objectives as we try to deal with these. Corporately, changing work demands often result in switching of personnel at mid-project—an excellent method for introducing inefficiency and losing continuity. These problems are unavoidable in some cases, but a clear focus on agreed goals and a solid commitment to achieving them can minimize their impact. Closely tied to this is the issue of prioritization. This is an important topic, which will be addressed in some detail later in this chapter.

I am somewhat obsessive about keeping to agreed deadlines. There has to be a very good reason for one to be missed—for example, my own death or something similar. Even then, I would seek agreement from the client to set a new delivery date. Having said this, I have recognized over the years that this commitment must be kept in balance like everything else. This was brought home to me a couple of years ago when I was hospitalized unexpectedly. I had promised a report to a client that week, and had only a few minor corrections to make to the draft; so from my hospital bed I gave instructions to my secretary to tidy up the report and issue it. When I got back to work a week later, I found that my boss had decided he wanted another chance to review the work before releasing it, and it had not been issued. We had missed the sacred deadline, and I was furious.

It took several weeks for me to begin to see the event in perspective. True, the report did not go out on the due date. However, the client already had the results of our work, and receiving the report "on time" would not have helped them implement our recommendations any sooner. The deadline was artificial. More important the client knew the circumstances, and was more concerned about my health than the delay of the report. All things in their right perspective!

Sort Your Priorities

As we have already seen, one major reason for failing to meet deadlines and achieve objectives is the uncontrolled intrusion of new demands. These can easily deflect us from the schedules we have set and the commitments we have made. At the same time, many of the new demands are legitimate. We are therefore placed in a dilemma: How do we sort out the conflicting demands, meet our agreed objectives, and save our sanity, all at the same time? The key is prioritization, and its basic canon is the Pareto principle or, as it is commonly called, the 80/20 principle. Stated simply, 80% of our results come from 20% of our activities. But how do we know which 20% to concentrate on? In the section that follows, we will examine a tool to help us.

A POWERFUL TOOL FOR PRIORITIZATION

Many writers on management and leadership have addressed the topic of time management and prioritization. John C. Maxwell[21] and Stephen R. Covey,[22] for example, both point out that we need to consider both *importance* and *urgency* when we set priorities.

The key point is that time-management decisions are two-dimensional. The dimension of urgency is a measure of time-sensitivity, and urgent things require immediate attention (e.g., selecting from a menu when you sit in a restaurant). The dimension of importance is a measure of consequence, and important things can have major long-term implications (e.g., choosing a major at college). The real killers are both urgent and important: they require immediate attention, and can have major long-term implications (e.g., the presentation this afternoon for your most important client).

I find it helpful to visualize this by plotting importance against urgency in a "Prioritization Plot" (Figure 2). These two parameters can both take any value between 0 and 100, where 0 is the lowest and 100 the highest.

The bottom section of the Prioritization Plot (the "Zero Band") represents the matters that we consider of little or no importance, and which therefore have values approaching zero in the scale of importance—no matter how "urgent" they may appear to be. These are the things that we choose to ignore or discard, like many of the special offers we receive in the mail, or junk e-mails that we delete, and so on. The rest of the space outside of the Zero Band represents the issues to which we choose to devote our time and attention.

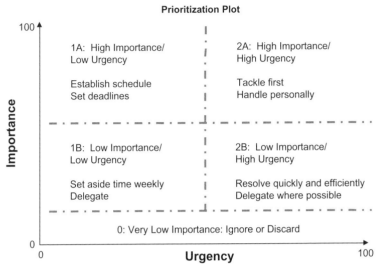

FIGURE 2   *Prioritization Plot*

Although importance and urgency can vary continuously between 0 and 100, it is a convenient simplification to assign values of either "high" or "low." This divides the space above the Zero Band in Figure 2 into four zones:

Zone 1A—High Importance/Low Urgency
Zone 2A—High Importance/High Urgency
Zone 1B—Low Importance/Low Urgency
Zone 2B—Low Importance/High Urgency

Whenever some new issue is brought to our attention, or a new demand is made on our time, our first task is to decide where it lies on the Prioritization Plot. This involves making a quick and efficient judgment of the importance and urgency that should be assigned in each case. Once we have made that determination for any particular matter we can decide how we will handle it. Over time situations may alter, new information may become available, or our opinion may change. We are then free to reclassify items and adopt new strategies for handling them.

Clearly, each type of demand has to be handled differently, and the Prioritization Plot is a very useful tool for deciding on an appropriate course of action. For example, key deadlines are important in the context of keeping to agreed project schedules. However, initially at least they are not urgent (High Importance/Low Urgency—Zone 1A). They can be anticipated and worked toward in a highly organized manner.

On the other hand, if a deadline is approaching and the required work is incomplete, the activity becomes urgent as well as important (Zone 2A). If the urgency becomes too great (approaching 100 on the urgency scale), this is a highly non-ideal situation. Many people go into panic under these circumstances, with highly adverse consequences to their projects. Having said that, some sense of urgency can be highly desirable. Without it, and the adrenalin that it produces, many people find it hard to be productive. If we find ourselves in a genuine Zone 2A situation, the Prioritization Plot is a powerful tool for sifting the other demands we face into those that have to be handled immediately and those that can be deferred until the "slack time" after the next deadline.

We should devote less effort to the less important tasks we face (Zones 1B and 2B). For example, while placing an order in a restaurant does require immediate attention (people are always anxious to be fed!), it does not usually warrant a major research project. It is clearly a Zone 2B activity (Low Importance/High Urgency) that should be handled quickly and efficiently. Other less urgent tasks (Zone 1B), like filing mail, can either be set aside until a convenient time or, if you have staff working for you, they can be delegated.

Too often our schedules are dominated by Zone 2A—things that are (or appear to be) both urgent and important. Many of these are crises that could have been averted with a little foresight and planning, while others are actually imposters—things that are perhaps not as important or as urgent as we are inclined to believe. Indeed almost everything that comes to us is presented as if it is a Zone 2A issue: the salesperson who wants you to buy the product today, the equipment that needs to be fixed immediately, the teenager who wants to borrow the car *now*. The ideal is to organize our lives and our work plans so that, as far possible, we work in Zone 1A—dealing with important issues at a sensible pace.

When I made this point in one of my seminars, one of the participants interjected, "My company operates in Zone 2A. We fight oilfield fires."

I did not give him a good response at the time, but I reflected on his observation after the seminar. Certainly Zone 2A is very much about fighting fires, both figuratively and literally. However, even firefighters do not spend all their time fighting fires. The bulk of their time is in fact spent *preparing* to fight fires: training, checking and maintaining equipment, planning. These are crucially important tasks, but they can generally be planned over a reasonable time frame—Zone 1A activities, in other words.

We need to be careful about how we assign items to the Zero Band. Once we have decided that something belongs in this category, we will most likely never consider it again, so it is generally worth checking twice before we finally press the delete button. A couple of years ago I received a suspicious-looking e-mail from overseas. At first I thought it was yet another Nigerian scam, but for some reason I read beyond the greeting line. That was when I realized that it was actually an invitation to teach a course in Malaysia. After an exchange of messages I accepted the invitation, and as a result I visited a country that I had never seen before, made new friends, and had a chance to grow professionally.

TIPS TO IMPROVE EFFICIENCY IN TIME MANAGEMENT

Having identified the general principles of time management and examined the Prioritization Plot, we turn now to consider a number of tips for effective time management. Some of these overlap, both with each other and with the material that we have already covered, and some seem to contradict one another. However, I have found all of these tips useful in a variety of situations.

Distinguish between What Is Essential and What Is Interesting

This special case of sorting priorities merits particular attention. It is very tempting to devote our time to pet projects and personal interests. This is especially true where we have a high degree of freedom to direct our own work.

We should not be employed in a job that does not involve substantial amounts of time devoted to things that we enjoy doing. However, if we simply follow these interests on a whim, the outputs from our work are uncertain and unlikely to be of great value. In most work situations this is not a particularly productive approach. We are generally far more productive if we have clearly defined objectives that we pursue in a disciplined manner—whether or not they happen to conform to our personal proclivities.

Identify Tasks and Set Milestones

An ancient Chinese proverb states that a journey of a thousand miles begins with the first step. That principle has wide-ranging applications. Setting overall objectives is laudable, but in practice most major goals—especially long-term ones—can only be accomplished through a series of much smaller "subgoals." For example, a college degree is obtained through a series of credits in a number of different courses, a book is written as a series of chapters, and all major projects have to be broken down into a series of discrete tasks.

At the beginning the ultimate goal looks daunting, but when it is broken down it becomes manageable. I no longer need to concern myself with the giant at the end of the road—only the dwarf on my doorstep. Moreover, breaking the tasks down and establishing milestones with specific deadlines helps in developing a strategy: I can see what I need to do and when I need to do it if I am to achieve my ultimate goal in the specified time. It also helps in identifying any additional resources that are required—for example, people whose input I will need, money, equipment—depending on the type of project. For small personal projects this can easily be done with pencil and paper. Software for scheduling and project management is a more appropriate tool for organizing work and tracking progress in larger projects that require inputs from many people.

By breaking down tasks and establishing milestones, I create a system for checking to ensure that I am doing the right things at the right times. Once the plan is in place—get on with it!

Avoid Perfectionism

Enormous amounts of time are spent on drafting and re-drafting documents, working and re-working presentations and trying, in every type of work, to achieve a "perfect" outcome. Much of this effort is wasted.

That is not to say that that some revisions are not desirable. It can be very helpful to get the opinion of a colleague before showing one's work to the world at large. Leaving a piece of work aside for a day or two and then returning to it can also lead to significant improvements. On several occasions when I have done that with reports that I had written, I found that I had difficulty understanding the message I was trying to convey. If I have difficulty understanding my own work, what chance does anyone else have? Revisions were in order.

However, efficiency demands the minimum of re-work. The goal in any job should be to get in right the first time—or as close to right as is reasonably possible. Endless changes—most of which are simply reflections of personal taste rather than anything of substance—are to be avoided.

Finish What You Start

Some multi-tasking is inevitable in all jobs. Unfortunately, this can lead to distractions that prevent the timely completion of important tasks.

There is no satisfaction in leaving tasks half done. As far as possible try to finish one job before moving on to another. Within organizations, one of the main causes of inefficiency is personnel changes in the middle of projects. Not only does this disrupt and delay the flow of work; it can also lead to frustration for the people involved.

For individuals, on a day-to-day basis smaller tasks should also be completed before moving on to something else. If a job is started and then left for any appreciable period, there is a significant loss of time involved in just remembering where you were, before any useful output is obtained.

Don't Create Crises

Many crises are the result of poor planning and a lack of anticipation. The student burning midnight oil the night before a major test is a phenomenon that we have all encountered—if not as the subject, then as the observer. It is surprising, though, how many mature professionals create similar situations for themselves—often to the intense annoyance of their secretaries, whose task it usually is to take care of the "rush job" that should have been done last week.

Don't Touch Any Piece of Paper More Than Once

The ideal is to deal with every issue as soon as it arises. For example, a fax arrives and needs a quick response, so write a short answer on the incoming fax. Reverse the "to" and "from" headings, and fax the reply back. Then get on with something else.

This approach works well with small tasks, especially those that have a degree of urgency. However, with bigger tasks, and especially those that require a significant amount of analysis or discussion, it is not realistic to make immediate decisions or take immediate actions. There is also a danger that if a lot of little tasks come in while you are trying to do an urgent big task, you could get distracted. A better option in this situation is to let the little tasks pile up for a while as you finish the urgent task. Then set aside time for a blitz on the pile, using the "one touch" principle.

List Tomorrow's Tasks at the End of Today

I have found that my days tend to be spent most efficiently if I have a current "to-do" list when I arrive in the office. This means that one of my last tasks in the evening is to prepare or update that list. For most people, it does not seem to work well to make a list first thing in the morning. One problem is that by then most of us have lost track of what we were doing the previous day. Another difficulty is that unless you come to work well before everyone else, there is usually quite a bit of activity when you get there. As a result you inevitably get sidetracked if you don't arrive with a predetermined game plan.

Don't Spend More Time on a Job Than It Warrants

Try to avoid spending more than the minimum of time on "low percentage" work—that is, tasks of uncertain importance. If the work is later determined to be important, more time can be allocated. However, there are no refunds on time after it has been spent.

Trust Your Intuition

Some people have the ability to reach conclusions (e.g., about technical matters, or about project management requirements) very rapidly, without being conscious of the underlying reasoning. This process is known as intuition, and it can be a very powerful tool in progressing work rapidly. Often the results reached by intuition are valid, and the logic behind the conclusions can be retraced—although retracing it may not be easy, and may take a long time.

There is nothing magical about intuition. It usually develops as people become fluent in a particular area, to the extent that they can anticipate an outcome from the beginning. Unfortunately, there is a tendency (especially among technical people) to be afraid of intuition because it seems unscientific and irrational. However, intuitive insights are often extremely useful for guiding more structured work. When intuition says that an answer is likely to be in a particular place, you should look there first. There is a good chance it is the right place, and you may save yourself a lot of time.

Beware of Meetings for the Sake of Meetings

Meetings of various types are inevitable in the working world, and they can be very productive. They can also be an amazing waste of time. A few key factors make the difference:

- *Agenda.* Any meeting must have a clearly defined purpose, and should be structured with that purpose in mind. There should be planned inputs (presentations, discussions, etc.)

leading to an anticipated output (e.g., a decision on a particular matter or a work plan).

- *People.* Given the agenda, who are the most appropriate people to attend? They are the ones who should be there; everyone else can probably be utilized more effectively elsewhere.
- *Atmosphere.* A balance needs to be maintained between the serious objectives of the meeting and the needs of the participants. A good laugh or two can provide a useful respite from heavy deliberations. Meetings should be fun! On the other hand, excessive levity can make it difficult to focus on the objectives of the meeting.
- *Leadership.* Whether it comes through a designated chairperson or simply from a strong individual, leadership is essential to make meetings work. The leader, by definition, is the person the others follow. This is the individual who ensures that the agenda is followed, and that the required deliverables come from the meeting.

Don't Work Too Many Hours

All of us have a work threshold beyond which extra time is nonproductive. Fatigue becomes a major factor after this point, and work becomes unfocused and ineffective. Moreover we all have responsibilities and interests away from work, and these also need some of our attention. This is the subject of a later chapter.

QUESTIONS FOR REFLECTION AND DISCUSSION

5.1. What are the main barriers that you personally experience in fulfilling the commitments you make and meeting schedule requirements?

5.2. What is the difference between urgency and importance? How good are you at distinguishing between them?

5.3. In the Prioritization Plot (Figure 2), which zone should occupy the bulk of our working time? Why?

5.4. What benefits can we obtain from identifying tasks and setting milestones?

5.5. The author warns us to "avoid perfectionism." Do you agree with this sentiment? How do you determine if a piece of work is "good enough"?

Chapter 6

Recognizing and Expanding Your Professional Limits

Noise proves nothing. Often a hen who has merely laid an egg cackles as if she has laid an asteroid.
—**Mark Twain**

I know nothing except the fact of my ignorance.
—**Socrates (quoted in Diogenes Laertius)**

To know that we know what we know, and that we do not know what we do not know, that is true knowledge.
—**Confucius**

All I know is what I read in the papers.
—**Will Rogers**

I have stated several times that professional excellence is *more* than technical competence. However, it is clear that there can be no true professional excellence *without* technical competence—and a technical competence that expands over time.

None of us can be an expert in everything, even within the limited realm of our own particular discipline. Professional work tends to be very specialized. For example, I have an architect friend who works almost exclusively in the design of car dealerships. I know another architect who specializes in designing churches. Neither of them would seek work in the other one's field, even though they are both qualified architects.

There are also legal and ethical issues to consider. Most professions have licensing requirements, which dictate the types of work that individuals can perform. For example, paragraph 137.59 of The Texas Engineering Practice Act and Board Rules[23] is headed "Engineers' Actions Shall Be Competent." It states, among other things, that "... Engineers shall practice only in their areas of competence . . . ."

So how do our competence and the limitations in our training affect us professionally? We consider several aspect of this in the present chapter.

DEVELOPING PROFESSIONAL COMPETENCE

Most of us had many years of formal academic training before entering the workforce. However, merely completing academic courses does not make us proficient in any professional field. It requires practical experience to apply the principles we learned in school and college to the practical situations we encounter as we progress in our careers. We become proficient through a *combination* of training and experience. For this reason professional licensing bodies generally have experience requirements in addition to academic requirements licensing bodies. For example, Professional Engineer license requirements in the State of Texas[24] include ". . . evidence . . . that the applicant has . . . engaged in the active practice of engineering" for a certain minimum number of years, depending on the applicant's other qualifications. The requirements in other disciplines and other jurisdictions are generally similar.

ACKNOWLEDGING LIMITS OF EXPERTISE

Quite apart from these legal issues, I have often found it necessary to tell clients that I personally could not advise on certain subjects, or that my company did not possess certain forms of expertise. Sometimes this has led me into disagreements with colleagues, especially those with sales responsibilities. There is a perception that candid acknowledgments of our limitations are bad for business. In practice, the exact opposite is usually true: *Acknowledging the limitations of our expertise often raises our credibility and enhances our ability to contribute.*

We lose credibility if we overstate our abilities and experience. Moreover we lose an important opportunity to build constructive relationships and team spirit. I have often been in meetings where an acknowledged "expert" has conceded ignorance in a certain field, and there was a perceptible easing of tension as soon as the admission was made.

OVERSTATING ACCOMPLISHMENTS

There is a great temptation for individuals and companies to overstate their accomplishments and capabilities in an effort to gain recognition or promote business. Of course, we all learned early in life that this is the wrong way to go about things. In his bestseller *All I Really Need to Know I Learned in Kindergarten*,[25] Robert Fulgum reminds us to "Play fair" and "Don't take things that don't belong to you." In the business world of adult life, these principles translate into honesty and integrity.

An incident that occurred quite early in my professional career confirmed to me that overstating accomplishments is both unwise and unnecessary. The incident involved a collaborative proposal for a government contract. I worked on this with several other people. The draft of one section of the proposal contained an untrue claim about the prior experience of one of the collaborators. We discussed this matter among ourselves on the team, and as a result the claim (just a few words, in fact) was removed. To my colleagues and myself the proposal looked weaker without the inaccurate claim; yet despite this we were awarded the contract. That led to a great deal of profitable work for us. Equally important (perhaps even more so), the work had high visibility, and gained us some very valuable recognition.

Several years later I met one of the government officials who evaluated our proposal. When he learned that I had been involved in writing it, he shook my hand and said, "It was the best proposal of its type I have ever seen."

Just recently I had an experience that further reinforced this principle for me. I met a prospective client for breakfast, and we discussed the client's need for help evaluating options in an oilfield project. I made it clear that even though I had some experience with the types of equipment he planned to use, that experience was in oil refining, not in oilfield development. As I left the client gave me a draft contract to review. We started working together the following week.

Of course, truthfulness does not guarantee success, but these incidents have reinforced my conviction that contrary to the opinion of some, it is the right strategy. Presenting an honest view of ourselves has many advantages, not least the fact that it avoids the risk of being caught in a lie. More important, though, it enables us to proceed with confidence and consistency, knowing that we have done all we can to ensure that our claims match up with reality.

Willful misrepresentation is plainly wrong. However, it is important to distinguish this from presenting myself or my company in the best light. We can legitimately focus on our strengths when we are selling our services—indeed that is exactly what we should do. For example, when we are asked for personal or business references, we go to our most satisfied employers or clients—not to the one or two who might be disgruntled. The problem comes when people or organizations "invent" personal or organizational strengths, qualifications, or experience in order to gain an advantage. Similarly it is important to distinguish between deliberate falsification and genuine errors. With the best will in the world mistakes happen. When they do the only policy I know is to acknowledge them, apologize, and correct them to the best of our ability.

At one of my seminars I quoted the old saying, "Honesty is the best policy." A member of the audience—a wonderful gentleman who has been in sales for more than 50 years—interrupted me. "No, sir, that's not right. Honesty is the *only* policy." I stand corrected.

EXPANDING PROFESSIONAL COMPETENCE

Personal and professional development should not stop when we enter our first job. We can and should expand our areas of professional competence. There are many opportunities to learn during a career—course work, on-the-job training, research. Many companies deliberately place new-hires in a wide range of varied job functions in the early years of their careers for precisely this reason. A broad understanding of company operations increases the employee's ability to add value over the course of his or her career. This process of expanding experience should always be done in a way that balances the individual's need for personal development with the requirements of adequate supervision and support, and with an understanding of the impact that frequent job changes have on ongoing projects.

As we take advantages of these opportunities, we can expand the limits of our professional competence. One of the joys of my own consulting work is the opportunity it offers to explore and develop new areas of process engineering. However, as I do this, it is sometimes necessary to make clients aware of the novel and tentative nature of the work.

QUESTIONS FOR REFLECTION AND DISCUSSION

6.1. What are the two main ways that we develop our professional competence and proficiency?

6.2. What benefits are obtained when people acknowledge to colleagues that they lack knowledge in certain areas?

6.3. "Honesty is the only policy." Do you agree with this statement? Why or why not?

6.4. The author distinguishes between "willful misrepresentation" and "presenting myself or my company in the best light." Do you agree with this distinction? What is the difference between the two types of representation?

Chapter 7

Investing in Your Profession and in Your Community

Ask not what your country can do for you; ask what you can do for your country.
—President John F. Kennedy, inaugural address, January 20, 1960.

No man is an island, entire of itself; every man is a piece of the continent, a part of the main.
—John Donne

Time and money spent in helping men do more for themselves is far better than mere giving.
—Henry Ford

In this fourth element of professional excellence we explore our interactions within our profession and with the broader community. Let's first consider why these interactions are important.

Professional Excellence: Beyond Technical Competence, by Alan Rossiter
Copyright © 2008 John Wiley & Sons, Inc.

A RATIONALE FOR INVESTING

As we saw in the last section, all professional disciplines require both a good academic grounding and a solid basis in practical experience. Each one of us has come as far as we have through a combination of our own determination to acquire these essentials and the help and encouragement that others have given us along the way. Each profession continues and progresses in large measure because of the willingness of its members to provide the same help and encouragement to those who follow.

Each profession also depends on its ability to make a positive contribution to society—and upon society's positive perceptions of what it does. As we perform our day-to-day work responsibly, our employers and the wider community benefit, both financially and in less tangible ways, from our professional efforts. However, the source of those benefits is often overlooked. By participating in activities that raise the visibility of our profession, we increase the community's appreciation of the contribution that our profession makes to our collective welfare.

This issue goes much further than the reputation of our professions, however. As we invest time and effort in our local communities, we raise the quality of life for all who live in them, and this provides very clear and direct benefits to ourselves and our families.

The term "community" has a broader application than our geographical neighborhood, especially in the era of globalization in which we live. Many professionals invest time, money, and effort in reaching out to disadvantaged groups either within their local area or in other parts of the world. This is generally motivated by humanitarian concern rather than any quantifiable gain that is obtained through these actions.

INVESTING IN YOUR PROFESSION

There are many ways in which we can invest in the furtherance of our profession. Here are a few of them:

> ***Participate in professional societies.*** Professional and technical societies, and trade associations, provide communities for

people in similar fields. These organizations often sponsor conferences, outreach programs, and other events that further the professions they represent. Many employers do similar things.

Introduce other people to your profession. Schools at every level are very happy when professionals in any field are willing to share their time with students. Over the years I have had many different opportunities of this type, starting with invitations to deliver occasional "industrial lectures" to undergraduates at a couple of universities shortly after I left university myself. Around the same time I was invited to participate in a program in which practicing engineers visited high schools to introduce students to the work we do. Other opportunities include judging science and engineering fairs and helping with "hands on" exhibits at museums.

Seize opportunities to help others grow in your profession. As our own experience grows, we are often placed in situations where we supervise other less experienced people. This provides a wonderful opportunity for professional development—both for ourselves and for the people we supervise. Teaching others enables us to learn far better than we can in any other way. There is also a great deal of satisfaction in this type of one-on-one professional interaction, especially as we see others grow professionally. In some cases it will be possible to expand this relationship beyond mere supervision or on-the-job instruction, and develop it into mentoring.

Be a mentor. Merriam-Webster's Dictionary[26] defines a mentor as a "trusted counselor or guide." The mentoring process works through a relationship between the mentor (a more experienced, mature, and successful person) and the protégé (a person new to the field or organization). The mentor gives guidance to the protégé in many areas, which might include knowledge, skills, career advancement, assimilation in the organization, and personal development. This relationship goes beyond formal instruction and includes the dimension of personal interaction. This aspect of mentoring can intimidate some people, and cause them avoid mentor/protégé relationships, but for many who do participate, the benefits are substantial.

Mentoring can be a win–win–win activity for the protégé, the mentor, and, if they both work for the same organization, for the organization too. Karen Beck[27] lists the following benefits for the different parties:

- The protégé gains not only a teacher but also the support of an influential friend and role model who can assist him or her in career development.

- The mentor can often learn new things (especially technical things) from the protégé, as well as increasing his or her value to the organization by helping to develop new employees. However, for most mentors the greatest benefit is the satisfaction of sharing knowledge and experience, and seeing the protégé develop.

- The organization benefits through more rapid assimilation and development of new employees, and better employee retention.

Karen also notes that mentoring relationships commonly go through four distinct phases, some of which are similar to the stages in a parent/child relationship:

- *Initiation.* At this stage (typically six months to a year) the relationship is focused on work tasks, with the mentor providing coaching to the protégé and promoting the protégé's visibility within the organization. Most mentoring relationships do not progress beyond this stage.

- *Cultivation.* During this phase, which typically lasts from one to five years, the mentor and protégé continue to work together, but the interactions become more frequent and personal, and an emotional bond develops.

- *Separation.* This occurs as a result of a structural change in the relationship. One party may move away, the protégé may be promoted or may desire greater autonomy (analogous to the adolescent child's desire to leave home), or there may be some type of negative personal interaction. Subsequent interactions between the parties may become hostile, leaving the mentor feeling hurt and unappreciated.

• *Redefinition.* Following separation, if the relationship is to be re-established, it must take on peer-like characteristics, similar to those of adult children and their parents. This is not always accomplished, but if it is, the hurt of the separation is diminished and replaced by feelings of gratitude and appreciation.

There is great satisfaction in seeing projects come to fruition as we work on them. But nothing compares with the satisfaction of seeing people develop positively, and knowing that we have been instrumental in some way to help them. Those who neglect this aspect of professional excellence miss a most rewarding experience.

Of course, not all of these opportunities are appropriate for everyone. Some people, including many excellent professionals, are not adept at lecturing or providing formal instruction—but they may be more comfortable in committee work within their professional societies or judging science and engineering fairs, for example. All of us can and should be willing to share the experience that we have gained to help those who come after us.

INVESTING IN YOUR COMMUNITY

Opportunities abound for professionals to contribute to society. This includes opportunities that are within our own neighborhoods, and others that are geographically far away. Some of these opportunities arise specifically because of our professional training and experience. Others are inherent in our membership of society.

Use Your Professional Abilities to Benefit Your Local Community

When we participate in projects professionally, each of those projects is intended to improve life in some way. Depending on our field, the project may involve a new bridge, a medical procedure, an audit report, a resolved lawsuit, a class that we have taught, or any number of other types of end product. One way or another, if we have performed our job responsibly, that end product improves the quality of life in our community. It is important that we understand this: our work is not just about making money for ourselves and our employers, although this is an important aspect of it. The bigger picture includes improvements in our community that come directly or indirectly from our professional work.

Quite apart from the work we are paid to do, our professional training and experience uniquely qualify us to carry out certain types of volunteer work within our local communities. For example, many lawyers perform *pro bono* legal work to assist nonprofit organizations or individuals who are financially unable to obtain adequate legal representation. Volunteer architects have an important role in organizations that seek to improve low-income housing. The skills of accountants are much sought after within charitable organizations that need help managing finances. Engineers, too, can apply their engineering skills within their local communities in a volunteer capacity. A few years ago I was at a PTO meeting, where a campus improvement was under discussion. The project involved construction of new walkways. Fortunately, one of the parents was a civil engineer, and he was able to advise the group on how to proceed with the project and evaluate bids.

Use Your Professional Abilities to Benefit the Wider Community

A few months ago I had dinner with a heart surgeon who led an American medical team on a two-week trip to Kenya. During the trip they performed more than a dozen surgeries for children who would otherwise not have been able to receive treatment for life-threatening conditions. The team members had to absorb a large part of the cost of the trip themselves.

I asked the doctor what motivated people like him to do this kind of work, and he told me that most of those who enter the medical field have a genuine desire to relieve suffering. Moreover there is a very special satisfaction in helping those who cannot help themselves. The contract that this particular surgeon negotiated with his current hospital includes specific language that ensures that he is free to perform a certain amount of voluntary work.

There are many organizations, many of them faith-based, that facilitate medical and dental teams visiting needy parts of the world, and judging from the number of people who participate in them, it is clear that the surgeon's assessment of his colleagues' motivation is correct. However, the spirit of service is not limited to the medical profession. There are many similar organizations and opportunities for professionals in other fields, such as teaching, agriculture, various branches of engineering, and business development, to name just a few. Many of the opportunities are short-term volunteer activities. However, some involve career changes and long-term relocations.

Explore Opportunities That Do Not Rely on Your Professional Background

A friend of mine—an engineer—has served for many years as volunteer financial manager for a low-income housing project. Other friends, with various professional backgrounds, have helped in the construction of some of the houses. Another engineer I know is a scoutmaster. These activities do not rely on the professional training of the individuals, and they illustrate how our ability to invest in our community transcends our formal training and our prior experience.

There are many such ways in which we can contribute. We can serve in positions that allow us to use our soft skills within our communities. This includes such things as coaching of youth sports programs, participation in school boards and parent groups, churches and other faith-based organizations, and local government. Which activities are best suited to each individual depends on personal circumstances and interests. The opportunities are limited only by our imagination.

QUESTIONS FOR REFLECTION AND DISCUSSION

7.1. Apart from your current studies and/or job, are you currently involved in any activities that invest in your profession? If so, what types of activities? Whether or not you are currently involved in activities that invest in your profession, do any of the types of activities listed in this chapter appeal to you? Are there any that you would like to try?

7.2. Have you ever had a mentor, or been a mentor? How do you feel about the experience? In particular, did you find it useful? Was it rewarding?

7.3. In what ways can people in your profession most readily use their professional skills to contribute to their local community?

7.4. Do you have any particular interests and/or skills outside of your professional area that you could apply to benefit your local community? (The chapter included examples such as youth sports coach and scoutmaster, but there are many other possibilities.)

7.5. The author emphasized the priority of helping those who cannot help themselves as a part of our contribution to society. What is your personal reaction to this idea?

Chapter *8*

Affirming Your Coworkers

I will speak ill of no man, and speak all the good I know of everybody.
—**Benjamin Franklin**

I can live for two months on a good compliment.
—**Mark Twain**

None of us can live or work in isolation. Our ability to "perform" in any area of life depends largely on the cooperation of those around us. Thus professional excellence must include the ability to evoke a cooperative spirit in the people who interact with us. This is best done by affirmation.

PERSPECTIVES ON COWORKERS AND SUBORDINATES

Consider the following two statements. The first comes from a plaque I saw on the wall of a colleague's office, and the second from an article in a technical journal:

People don't do what you expect. They do what you inspect.

—Anonymous

If you want to get people to do more, raise your expectations.

—Doug Hissong[28]

What do these statements tell us about the attitudes of the respective authors toward their colleagues and workplace subordinates?

The first statement conveys the idea that most people dislike work, and will avoid it if they can. They lack ambition, avoid responsibility, require direction for every action, and want security above all else. Managers have to use threats in order to get employees to work toward organizational objectives.

The second statement conveys a very different perception of people. It says that they naturally want to excel, if they are given the chance and the confidence to do so. Most people can pursue organizational goals without external control or threats, and they usually accept and often seek responsibility. Many people have the ability to use imagination, creativity, and ingenuity to solve organizational problems, and too often their intellectual potential is underutilized.

You may recognize many of these themes from our discussion in Chapter 1 of Abraham Maslow and his research on human potential. However, these two distinctive viewpoints on workplace behavior are more fully developed by Douglas McGregor in his 1960 book, *The Human Side of Enterprise.*[29]

McGregor is perhaps best-known for the classic X-Y theory of management. Type X managers are authoritarians. They are generally results-oriented, and do not understand or have an interest in human issues. By contrast, Type Y managers take a participative approach—that is, they look for greater dialogue with employees, aim to treat people as people rather than cogs in an industrial machine, and encourage others to develop to their full potential. McGregor strongly advocated the Type Y approach to management. The Type Y management style builds a cooperative spirit, and affirmation is a key component to this. The Type Y manager conveys to his people that they are capable of accomplishing more than they are doing, and as a result they achieve more.

What is affirmation? Basically it is helping others to feel good about themselves and the contribution they are making. This is an important application of the principle of consideration and respect for the other person that was introduced in Chapter 2.

APPLICATIONS OF AFFIRMATION

The applications of affirmation are many, covering virtually every field of human activity. One of the most striking examples that I have seen was in my elder son's football team when he played as a thirteen-year-old. The team lost their first three games, and the boys were becoming despondent. The coach, however, did not berate them. Rather, he repeatedly told them that he knew that they had ability and that they could do better, and he kept up a rigorous practice program. The boys responded by working hard. They had a week off after their third game, and when they returned for the fourth game, they won handsomely. They continued to win all their games for the rest of the season until the league championship match, which they narrowly lost.

Was the team's turnaround entirely because of the coach's encouragement? Probably not. There was a lot of talent in the team, but a few key injuries early in the season affected their initial performance. The improved performance coincided with the key players returning to full strength. However, it would have been easy for the boys to lose heart after their initial setbacks, and the coach's exhortations prevented that. To me, that coach will forever be the embodiment of affirmation.

Words of appreciation and encouragement have a very positive impact. When things are going well, affirmation can be an expression of appreciation and praise for those who contributed to the success. When your team or an individual in it has suffered a disappointment or setback, affirmation is the reassurance that there will be a rebound. The goal is, one way or another, to convey a sense of value and appreciation to others. If instead we adopt attitudes that convey the impression that the people around us have little to offer, we isolate ourselves, hinder the development of team spirit, and ultimately reduce our effectiveness.

We can apply this principle in many ways within our professional lives. The most obvious area of application is in our dealings with our immediate juniors, but bosses need affirmation too. Also, what about the taxi driver who takes you to an important meeting, or the waiter who serves you while you are away from home on business? All of these people contribute to our professional performance, and we help them help us through affirmation.

NEGATIVE EXPERIENCES

Not all of our experiences are positive. A friend of mine worked as an accountant with a large firm. After 20 years with the company he was transferred at a fairly senior level to new division. Immediately he encountered problems. The particular incident that he recounts involved a meeting that included a number of his peers and his supervisor. During the meeting my friend made a suggestion to change a certain procedure. His supervisor immediately responded by saying, "That's the most ridiculous idea I ever heard."

Was the idea ridiculous? I don't know. However, the supervisor's ridicule in the presence of a group of peers was humiliating to my friend. If his suggestion really was bad, and if the supervisor felt it necessary to draw my friend's attention to this, the right course of action would have been to discuss the matter in private. It is hard to believe that the supervisor was not aware of this, and my friend concluded that for some reason the supervisor and others disliked him, and wanted him to leave. If so, they succeeded. A few months after this incident he took a job with a small company in a different industry.

Sometimes we do need to correct people, or to make comments that may not appear positive. How we go about this is important—for example, talking to people privately rather than publicly, as discussed in the previous paragraph. However, our relationships with people are also crucially important. I have heard from several people that the negative emotional impact of a single criticism is seven times as great as the positive impact of a word of praise. I have also heard that relationships can survive with 20% of negative content provided that the other 80% is positive. I have never been able to verify these statistics, but they feel about right. The point is that if we can be generally positive and affirming in our dealings with others, they are more likely to respond well when we do have to correct them, or if some aspect of our dealings becomes difficult.

TIPS ON AFFIRMATION

In affirmation, our goal is to convey a sense of value, acceptance, reassurance and appreciation to others. There are many different ways this can be done, for example:

> ***Remember to thank people when they do something for you.*** It is very easy to fall into the trap of complaining when people don't come up to expectations, and ignoring them when they deliver. If we are to elevate the people around us, we need to be generous with our positive comments whenever an opportunity arises. We should constantly be looking for the chance to say uplifting things at home, at work, or wherever we are.
>
> ***Use small gifts, cards, notes, or e-mails to convey appreciation, condolence, or encouragement.*** There are many different vehicles that we can use to provide affirmation. Which one we select depends on the specific situation and the nature of our relationship with the individual or individuals concerned.
>
> ***Apply affirmation both individually and corporately.*** The same principles that apply to the affirmation of one individual by another can also be adapted for groups—for example, a manager affirming a team. Small gifts distributed to the group to celebrate a success or even "just because" can be a good way to encourage people and build morale.
>
> ***View other people positively.*** We noted earlier in this chapter that the goal of affirmation is to help others to feel good about themselves and the contribution they are making. If we are to do that consistently, we must have a positive view of the people around us. If we see all people as inherently valuable, or as being made in God's image, we will find that affirmation is a natural extension of that outlook. From these perspectives all people warrant our consideration *regardless* of their impact on us professionally or personally. On the other hand, if we see people as things to be used for our

convenience, affirmation is an unnatural response that will be difficult to apply with any consistency.

Use genuine compliments. The goal of affirmation is to build on people's positive attributes and performance. Positives exist in all people. The first task of affirmation is to identify those positives for the person we wish to affirm. We then need to make that individual aware that we have noticed those positives—in other words, compliment them. When people feel good about the positive things they have done, they will be more inclined to do them again.

Use repartee—but only when appropriate. Verbal jousting and wordplay within a group of friends or coworkers may appear negative—even insulting—to outsiders, but it can be very affirming to those within the group. It can also be great fun. Inclusion in the thrust and parry of repartee is a sign of acceptance. However, this particular form of affirmation has to be used with care. More than once I have offended people with my banter, and I am not the only person who has made that error. There needs to be a level of familiarity among people for this most peculiar type of affirmation to work.

QUESTIONS FOR REFLECTION AND DISCUSSION

8.1. Think about the teachers and supervisors that you have studied and worked under. Did any of them show the characteristics of Type X or Type Y managers? How do you personally respond to the two different management styles?

8.2. What is the goal of affirmation? Why is it important to affirm coworkers and other people with whom we interact?

8.3. The author describes a situation where affirmation and encouragement by a coach turned the season around for his son's football team. Have you personally experienced the positive results of affirmation and encouragement? If so, describe the experience.

8.4. List three methods that can be used for affirming coworkers.

Chapter 9

Celebrating Your Work

Enjoy your achievements as well as your plans.
—***Max Ehrmann,*** **Desiderata**

You have no more right to consume happiness without producing it than to consume wealth without producing it.
—***George Bernard Shaw,*** **Candida, I**

The most wasted of all days is one without laughter.
—***E.E. Cummings***

A memory that stands out from my early years in industry was an encounter with a senior colleague who had just been promoted. I casually asked how he was enjoying his new responsibilities. He grunted and said, "I'm not," and walked off. How sad.

The work we do carries a lot of responsibility. It can be very demanding. Parts of it are frankly tedious. If we are to survive emotionally, it is essential that we maintain a good balance, and don't take ourselves too seriously—not all the time, anyway. A sense of the absurd and a spirit of fun and celebration should be an integral part of our daily work.

THE ROOTS OF CELEBRATION

The practice of celebrating the results of human labor goes back to the most ancient of times—to the hunter celebrating his kill, and the farmer's festival after bringing in the harvest. The concept is also embodied in some very ancient literature.

In the Hebrew account of the Creation, at the end of each day of creative activity, God sat back and reviewed what he had accomplished with satisfaction. For the first five days He declared his work "good." On day six, it was "very good" (Genesis 1:31).

On day seven, He rested (Genesis 2:2). Why? Was He tired? No! The God of Genesis does not get tired. So what was He doing? Simple. The context makes it clear that He was reflecting and celebrating, enjoying His creation.

The Creation account highlights a principle that has been embedded in the work environment as far back as human records go. It transcends cultures and creeds. The principle is this: there is a cycle of work and celebration.

DIMENSIONS OF CELEBRATION

The principle of celebration has a wide range of applications, both individually and corporately. We explore these two dimensions below, and see the positive effect that having fun can have.

Celebrate Individually

It is easy to be overwhelmed by work, especially when our objectives take a long time to reach. One way to counter this is to reflect positively on our progress each day, each week, and at each significant milestone—for example, at the completion of a project. At its most basic level this can be achieved by keeping a task list, and checking off each item as you complete it. The task list is in itself a tool for structuring work, as discussed in an earlier chapter, but there is also a measure of satisfaction in the act of recording the completion of a task ("it was good"), no matter how small the task may seem.

At the completion of a larger project we should allow ourselves time to relax and look back with satisfaction, perhaps spend some time with friends in a favorite pastime, and declare to ourselves and others, "It is very good!"

Celebrate Together

Group celebrations can take different forms, both informal and formal. Informally, coworkers often get together for meals or other activities to celebrate. On the formal side, many companies apply the principle of celebration as part of team building. There are numerous ways this can be done, for example:

- Take advantage of holiday seasons for company festivities
- Mark each completed project with a token of accomplishment. These might include:
  - ➢ Plaques
  - ➢ Photos
  - ➢ Special items of clothing
  - ➢ Souvenirs

Whether the activity is formal or informal, the key is to find satisfaction in our accomplishments, have fun, and build positive memories

Have Fun

I experienced a striking example of the fun aspect of this while I was in Japan a number of years ago. I had been conducting a seminar, and on the last day I helped the Japanese secretary tidy up the equipment we had been using for computer demonstrations. We loaded some boxes on a cart, and then she told me to get on too. I did. She then pushed the cart down the corridor, in full view of the entire office staff. We must have looked like a couple of kids playing. Formality was gone, and everyone who saw us fell about laughing. It was wonderful.

Fun is all about spontaneity and the dropping of unnecessary inhibitions. Of course, this must not lead to crude, distasteful, or dangerous behavior. But an office or a lecture hall, or even a construction site or a control room, without laughter and enjoyment is a dead place, and we do ourselves and those around us a great disservice if we stifle it.

Some time ago a young engineer from a client's organization came into the office where a colleague and I were working, and announced: "I've never met anyone who enjoys their work as much as you two." I took that as a profound compliment.

QUESTIONS FOR REFLECTION AND DISCUSSION

9.1. What negative aspect or aspects of work can be countered by celebration?

9.2. Do you use any techniques to maintain a positive attitude to your work? If so, what are they?

9.3. List as many ways as you can that companies can apply the principle of celebration to help build team spirit. Try to identify options that are not listed by the author.

9.4. What benefits are there in having fun at work? Can you identify any dangers in having fun at work?

Chapter *10*

Protecting Your Personal Life

The best and safest thing is to keep a balance in your life, acknowledging the great powers around us and in us. If you can do that, and live that way, you are really a wise man.
—Euripides

I've learned that you can't have everything and do everything at the same time.
—Oprah Winfrey

Few people who have led successful lives have also achieved the most important success of all, namely of being a good father and taking part in the joys and extra dimensions that a close relationship with one's family can give.
—Sir John Harvey-Jones, MBE, former chairman, Imperial Chemical Industries, plc (ICI)

Happiness is having a large, loving, caring close-knit family in another city.
—George Burns

The test of the morality of a society is what it does for its children.
—Dietrich Bonhoeffer

Life is not all about work. What we do outside of work, and the commitments we take on, are very individual, but we all have and need some kind of life outside of the workplace. Earlier chapters included discussions on our responsibility to invest in our communities, and on the benefits of spending some time away from work to keep a right perspective on things. There is also a more personal responsibility to ourselves and our families, and this is the subject of the present chapter. Work has a habit of encroaching on these other areas, and it is essential that we maintain a right balance between the conflicting priorities that arise.

FITNESS AND HOBBIES

It is important that we strive to maintain physical and mental health to the extent that we can. Regular exercise is crucial for a healthy lifestyle. It has clear benefits in physical fitness and the resulting quality of life, and it also provides an emotional outlet that can be helpful in relieving stress. Many people also report that exercise provides other benefits, including an improved sense of well-being, increased productivity at work, and better sleep at night.

Since my teens I have enjoyed running, and that is still how I get most of my exercise. There has been an upsurge in recent years in organized road running, from local 5K events to ultra-marathons, and this has made running a very popular way for professional people to stay physically fit. Many fitness organizations have grown up with this trend, so it is now very easy to join a running group. Typically these groups provide both coaching and camaraderie, which help participants to stay involved. Some also include the dimension of fund-raising for charities by seeking sponsors for runners. The most prominent example is The Leukemia and Lymphoma Society's "Team in Training" organization, which claims to be the world's largest endurance sports-training program.[30]

However, running isn't necessarily the right thing for everyone. One of the key elements of a successful physical fitness program is that it should be enjoyable. If it is not enjoyable, then it is very difficult to maintain enthusiasm and commitment to the program. Personal preference should therefore be a major factor in selecting physical fitness activities. These might include swimming, tennis, or gym workouts, or simply walking (with or without your dog), for example. Fitness activities that include a social dimension are often more sustainable because of the mutual encouragement that takes place among the participants.

A word of caution: A person who has not engaged in strenuous physical exercise for an extended period should get a medical checkup before starting an exercise program. Furthermore, if exercise results in significant discomfort, you should stop and seek advice.

Hobbies, cultural interests, and other forms of recreation are also beneficial. Apart from the enjoyment they provide, activities of this type often provide opportunities to make friends from outside of the normal work and home environment, which helps to keep us balanced. Some of these activities are intellectually stimulating, while others are intended to be purely relaxing; some are for you alone, while others might include family members or friends. Once again, the choice of activities comes down to personal preference.

FAMILY AND FRIENDS

The relationships we form demand time and attention. Family and friends enrich any life, but they can also be very demanding on time and resources. It is important that we make appropriate allowances for this.

I have found the following three principles particularly helpful for protecting these relationships while pursuing an interesting and stimulating career:

> *Communicate.* This topic was presented earlier as the first element of professional excellence. The discussion there focused mainly on communication in the work environment. In the present context, however, the focus is communication with friends and family members, and the balancing of personal commitments and work demands. In dealing with this balance, it is important that we should be open and honest in expressing the problems we are experiencing. When we

understand the pressures that others are experiencing, and they understand our situation, it is usually possible to develop workable compromises and resolve conflicts. This concept is important in all relationships—at home, at work and in any other area where we are active.

Failure to apply this principle can lead to misunderstandings and conflict in the workplace and the home. This was highlighted for me a few years ago, when I went overseas on a short assignment. As soon as I arrived I was asked to extend my stay. However, I had made a number of personal and professional commitments based on my returning immediately after the assignment, and I declined to stay on. There followed a period of tension between myself and the top management of my company.

The real problem, of course, was a failure to communicate effectively. We were probably all at fault. For my part, I did not check the requirements of the assignment carefully enough before agreeing to do it. I had done similar things many times before, and I assumed that this one would be organized like the previous ones. My company's management, on the other hand, assumed that I would anticipate a need to stay beyond the "official" end of the assignment. It is very dangerous to replace proper communication with assumptions!

Prioritize. We discussed prioritization principles for work in Chapter 5. However, no matter how urgent the demands of the job, we must also make time to fulfill our other commitments to family and friends, and to relax and recover our sense of perspective. In the parlance of the Prioritization Plot, these are Zone 1A activities—high importance, low urgency. This means that we must block out time on our calendar for them. For example, we could:

➢ Get a season subscription to the theater with a spouse
➢ Arrange to meet friends regularly for lunch or at a sporting event
➢ Set aside time for weekly worship services as a family

Reciprocate. It is unfair and unreasonable for one party to inconvenience another all the time. This is especially true of "two career households," which are now so common. The

CHILDREN IN THE LIFE OF THE PROFESSIONAL **85**

demands of one person's work often result in added burdens for the other person. For example, if a husband has to spend a lot of time away from home due to his work, it may require his wife to serve double duty taking care of children and managing all household tasks. It is only fair and reasonable that the husband should also accept additional duties when he is able—perhaps looking after the children for a while to allow his wife to pursue outside interests.

More generally, it can greatly ease tensions in domestic situations when duties are shared equitably. Especially where one partner is the major wage-earner, there is a tendency for that person to opt out of most domestic chores. This can quickly lead to resentment. If that individual accepts at least some responsibilities—loading the dishwasher after meals, for example—it creates a sense of partnership and goodwill.

CHILDREN IN THE LIFE OF THE PROFESSIONAL

A few weeks ago I received an instant message from a friend in Malaysia. He and I are working on a project together. He told me that he would have to adjust his schedule a bit for the month of January because he and his wife are expecting their first child then. I responded that the schedule changes would probably last longer than just one month. The instant messaging after that went something like this:

"How much longer?"

"At least 18 years"

At that point there was a lengthy delay in his response. I think he must have fallen off his chair. When he did reply, it was to say:

"I'd like to know more on what you have to say about child-rearing."

I had to leave at that point, so I never gave him a proper response on this subject—but I have thought a lot about it. Not all of the readers of this book have children at home. For some, this is an experience that lies in the future; for others, a phase in the past.

There are yet others who, either by choice or for reasons beyond their control, will never go through a child-rearing chapter in their lives. However, for those who do combine child-rearing with a professional career this is a very important topic, so I feel it appropriate to address this in the pages that follow.

The arrival of children has a major impact on our lifestyle, even more than marriage does, and the issues are complex. Children differ greatly. My wife and I have two teenage sons, one of whom is very "easy" and the other very "difficult." What works in parenting one of them often doesn't work for the other.

Many books have been written on the subject of parenting, and I have read quite a few of them over the years, looking for solutions to problems that we have encountered. One of the main difficulties that I have found while doing this is that the experts disagree in many key areas, which only adds to the confusion of struggling parents.

An incident a few months ago highlighted for me the difficulties experienced by the experts themselves. I attended a seminar on raising teenagers, and there in the audience I met a friend who is a child psychologist and family therapist. She also happens to have a son about the same age as one of my boys.

"What brings you here?" I asked. "I thought you taught seminars like this, rather than just sitting in the audience."

"Yes," she said, "but it is very different when it's your own kids that you are dealing with."

Her response reminded me of the pastor who described his family counseling work this way: "When I started as a pastor I had no children, but I had four principles of child-rearing that I used. Now I have four children, and no principles." If the "experts" have such difficulty, what hope is there for the rest of us?

All is not lost. Parents have been raising children (and making mistakes in the process) for thousands of years, and human society has not collapsed. I certainly don't have all the answers, but I would like to close this section by summarizing a few ideas on child-rearing. This starts with three general principles (despite the pastor story that I just shared), and continues with a number of applications.

Principle 1: Keep the Goal in Mind

In the day-to-day activities of parenting it is easy to forget why we are doing what we do. However, when we look at things objectively, it is clear that our primary responsibility as parents is to equip our children as they grow, with the ultimate goal of producing responsible young adults.

Children are constantly changing—growing, developing. At each stage in the growing process they need support. This becomes strikingly apparent as children enter their teens and the time approaches for them to claim their rightful independence. We are approaching that situation in my household, and there is a strong sense of the necessity to prepare our boys for adulthood. However, they also need support at each of the earlier steps in their development.

In the early years the parenting role is concentrated in meeting basic needs of feeding, clothing, and cleaning. As time goes on, we quickly find that we are guiding our children through social interactions with family members and friends, teaching them arithmetic and spelling, and coaching their sports—preparing then to succeed socially, academically, and athletically. Then, before we quite realize it, we are helping them prepare for college.

Yet, looking back on the years, the most important constant is that—often unconsciously—we as parents are continually transmitting our values and our attitudes to our children. This is the most important of all forms of preparation for the future.

I live in Texas, so naturally I listen to a lot of country music. One song that is currently quite popular is Rodney Atkins's *Watching You*.[31] It describes the experiences of a father and his four-year-old son. The father had to brake suddenly while they were driving together. The boy spilled his food and drink and "said a four letter word (that) started with S." When the father asked him where he had learned to talk like that, the lad told him, "I've been watchin' you."

When they returned home the father went to the barn to pray that he might be a better example to his boy. Later that evening he watched the boy praying to God "like he was talkin' to a friend," so he asked him, "Now where'd you learn to pray like that?" The answer, of course, was, "I've been watchin' you."

What attitudes and values am I conveying to my boys? Regrettably, like Rodney Atkins, I know they have not always been positive ones, but I hope that most of them have been. Those attitudes and values are a big part of what will shape the type of men they become.

Principle 2: Enjoy the Moment

Recognizing the weight of responsibility the comes with parenthood can be overwhelming, especially when it is combined with the other burdens of life. It is very easy to loose perspective, especially when we encounter discipline problems, lack of gratitude, or apparent unresponsiveness from our children. When this happens, it is easy to grow discouraged, and parenting can become a joyless occupation.

Yet in the midst of the fray, there are priceless moments. A few months ago my younger son was in the final of his school's "Math Counts" competition. The event was held in the school library and televised on the school's closed circuit TV system, so my wife and I went to the school office to watch. After a titanic battle our lad took second place, and when the event finished we waited with the crowds outside the library for him to appear. When he did, he and I fell into each other's arms laughing and crying. Most things you can buy with MasterCard, but that was priceless! Whatever struggles we may have had with our kids (and there have been many), nothing can take that away from me.

Principle 3: Use All Your Skills

The skills and techniques used in child-rearing are closely linked to several of the other elements of professional excellence that I described earlier. This really is not surprising. Children are people too, after all.

- We need to understand them, and they need to understand us. In short, there needs to be effective communication between parent and child.
- They need stability, the assurance that they will not be abandoned. It is therefore very important that we fulfill our commitments to them.

- They crave the attention and approval of their parents. This is the main mechanism for developing self-esteem, and if we neglect this, it we can cause serious harm. This is a very important application of the principle of affirmation.

With these principles in mind, here are some specific applications that I have found useful. Perhaps they will also help my friend in Malaysia, and others who read this.

Make Time for Your Child

Spending time with a child is a great form of affirmation because it conveys the sense that the parent places importance on being with the child. It also provides a framework for communication between parent and child.

I have seen a lot of debate on whether the "quality" of the time we spend with our children is more important than the "quantity" of the time we spend. I have come to the conclusion that the question is irrelevant. Children demand time from mom and dad, and lots of it ("quantity"). The value ("quality") of that time is much less tangible. Priceless moments come and go unpredictably. Patrick Morley[32] recounts an all-day father and son fishing trip. The son was Boswell, the famous biographer of Samuel Johnson. In later years Boswell recalled that fishing trip as one of the most memorable and wonderful experiences of his childhood. The entry for that day in his father's diary, however, reported it as "a day wasted." In the evaluation of parent-child activities, the child's assessment is more important than the parent's.

The main task of parents in this area is to find suitable ways to spend time with their children. When the children are very young, this happens quite naturally because their moment-by-moment needs for feeding and diaper changing require constant adult intervention. As time goes on, though, they become more independent, and we need to look for new ways to interact. Opportunities abound,[33] although which options are most appropriate depends greatly on the personal circumstances of the parents. For younger children visits to the zoo or park are often suitable. As they grow, the opportunities include coaching your child's sports teams, camping trips and family vacations, and simpler things like a spontaneous trip to the movies or just playing games (board games, card games, even video games) at home. It is also a good idea to keep at least one meal per day as a time for a family gathering.

It helps a great deal if the parent and child have a common interest—and of course, as parents we often introduce our children to our own interests anyway. For example, my younger son and I often play chess together, and both of our boys have joined me in road running events. I have also tried weekend biking with my elder son, and I declare the experiment a partial success. Because of time conflicts we only managed a few rides together, but they were fun times that combined exercise with a chance to get to know each other better.

In addition to sharing common interests, it is important for parents to stay involved in their children's school activities and any other programs in which they participate, such as sports. This provides a mechanism for parents to stay in touch with the teachers, coaches, and other significant adults in their children's lives (more on this later), as well as with their children's peers. It also conveys to the children that their parents care about them, and it can be very rewarding for the parents too.

I try to spend a few minutes of quiet time with each of my children each day, usually just before they go to bed. Unfortunately, this doesn't always happen because of my travel commitments and other factors, but more often than not it does. When they were very young, this was the time for bedtime stories. Now they are teenagers, it is more likely to be a general chat time—something that the younger boy, in particular, really seems to enjoy. Usually nothing outwardly important happens during these times, but occasionally something very significant surfaces—a difficulty at school or with a friend, or some other problem the child is dealing with. Unless the parent and child spend (and apparently waste) a lot of time together ("quantity"), these significant times ("quality") would never happen.

Find Ways to Say Yes

Children do need boundaries, and most parents start very early in setting these. This commonly involves repeated use of the word "no" when the child starts throwing food on the floor, or displays similar antisocial behavior. As time goes on, children often make unreasonable requests—the toddler asking for the thirteenth bowl of ice cream today, or the teenager wanting to take the car on an eighty mile per hour rampage through the neighborhood. The word "no" quickly becomes a reflex response. However, not all of the things children want are unreasonable. It is important therefore to look for opportunities to provide at least some things that our children really want.

This does not mean that we should spoil them. Most things in life do not come easily, and that is an important lesson for children to learn. But when we say "yes" to some of the reasonable requests that they make, we are conveying our love and understanding. This is an important part of building trust and goodwill.

Be Quick to Praise

Parents are charged with disciplining their children, and we tend to be quick to notice and reprimand when they do something wrong. Unfortunately, too often we forget even to comment when they do things right. The fact is that even the most disobedient or inept child does do a lot of things right, and when we praise them for it, the positive feedback encourages them to do more things right. This is the essence of affirmation.

Like many parents of teenagers, we are going through the "learning to drive" phase right now with my older son. It is a nerve-racking experience, and it is very hard not to point out the many deficiencies in his judgment when he is at the wheel. I try (not always successfully) to hold my tongue when he is a little off, but when he executes a smooth turn or some other good maneuver I try to remember to say "nicely done," or something similarly positive.

Take All the Help You Can Get

Hillary Clinton popularized the saying, "It takes a village to raise a child." The concept is right. Even with two parents in the home child-rearing is demanding, exhausting work, and the burden is even greater for single parents. We need a break from time to time. Added to that there are things that children will confide in other trusted adults that they won't tell their parents, even if the parent-child relationship is good. Yet other adults can encourage them and build their self-esteem in ways that their parents cannot.

Teachers, coaches, scoutmasters, youth leaders, and others who spend time with our children are all potential allies in the great work of child-rearing, and we have been privileged to have had a number of these people take a positive interest in our boys over the years. As parents, we try to maintain as much contact as we can with these important adults (e.g., by being involved in school activities), to encourage them in their work. Also, by maintaining good communication, we can help each other identify and head off problems that our kids are facing as they arise.

There are also professionals who have been trained to deal with the specific issues and problems of parenting and child development. This includes pastors, family therapists, and other mental health specialists, and there are situations where it is appropriate to seek out help from experts in these fields. They can be great allies. However, their work can never be a substitute for parental involvement.

Say "No" to Guilt

The behavior of our children often falls short of what we might hope, and outcomes are not always what we would like. Many parents feel that this is their fault, and they struggle with guilt as a result. Parents can also feel overwhelmed by all that they are expected to do for their children, and become discouraged when they find that they can't do it all. Friends, family, and colleagues, as well as people in authority and the family down the street that apparently "has it all together," can also make us feel inadequate, either deliberately or unintentionally.

I have one simple response: Don't submit to this. Parenting is a difficult job, but it gets much harder if the parents are struggling with guilt. It is also worth noting that, contrary to appearances, the family down the street isn't quite perfect either. While struggling with our own difficulties, we just don't see theirs. Perfectionism is a terrible taskmaster!

The Canadian poet, author and singer/songwriter Leonard Cohen expressed this principle well in his *Anthem*:[34]

Ring the bells that still can ring

Forget your perfect offering

There is a crack in everything

That's how the light gets in.

Perhaps now my friend in Malaysia will understand why the arrival of his first child in January will affect his schedule for more than a month. Raising children is a demanding, challenging enterprise. It is also one of the most important and rewarding jobs in the world. It should not be considered inferior to the other jobs we do. It affects the way we do our professional work, and the way we view our world.

QUESTIONS FOR REFLECTION AND DISCUSSION

10.1. Do you participate in sports or other activities that help you to keep physically fit? If you do, what is your favorite activity of this type, and why? If not, is there any sport that you have enjoyed in the past? What would be required for you to take this up again—or are there other exercise activities that you would prefer to try now?

10.2. Apart from physical fitness, what other benefits do people derive from regular exercise?

10.3. Briefly explain the principle of reciprocation in protecting your personal life.

10.4. How do you handle conflicts between work priorities and the demands of family and friends?

10.5. The author comments that many of the same principles that result in excellence in the workplace are also applicable in our personal lives. Do you have personal experiences that either support or refute this claim? Give examples and explanations.

Epilogue: Nothing Lasts Forever

6 pm, Thursday, March 12, 1992. I had just put the vegetables into the microwave for supper. I closed the microwave door and looked at the controls—but I couldn't figure out which button to push. Then I noticed that it was difficult to keep my balance, so I clutched at the countertop. My wife, who was playing in the lounge with Daniel (then just one year old), looked up in alarm and asked if anything was wrong. I tried to answer but couldn't, so I simply nodded my head. Then, realizing that my legs beneath me suddenly felt very weak, I lay on the floor to preempt a fall.

Seeing me on the floor meant only one thing to Daniel: Daddy wants to play!! He ran to me from the lounge just as quickly as his little legs would carry him, laughing all the way. Daddy sorely wished he could have played. Instead, I tried weakly to reach out my arms to embrace the lad, but I couldn't; and at that moment I experienced an emotional flood that was unique in my experience. The closest I can come to describing it is to call it bereavement— the sense of having lost someone immensely dear to me, although it was my own death that was in prospect. Only recently we had celebrated Daniel's first birthday; would I still be there to celebrate

Professional Excellence: Beyond Technical Competence, by Alan Rossiter
Copyright © 2008 John Wiley & Sons, Inc.

his second? Would I see him off on his first day at "big school"? Would I be there proudly watching him as a young man, setting off to make his mark on the world? Hope ebbed, and grief took its place.

The next day found me in an intensive care unit in a major hospital, bedridden, heart monitor making its rhythmic trace, IV stuck in my arm. Not a pretty sight. Over the next few days they carried out a battery of tests on me, and I learned quite a bit about high-tech nondestructive testing methods for the human body and brain.

I am a Christian, and I can honestly say that my relationship with my Lord has never been more comfortable than it was in those days in hospital. I had often wondered how I would react when confronted by death. My situation presented that very real possibility, and with it a perhaps more daunting alternative—lifelong paralysis. Yet during those days of uncertainty, apart from a couple of brief aberrations, I felt no dread on my own behalf. What I did feel was a compelling concern for my wife and my young son, and the continuing sense of grief that I might not be around to see him grow.

The verdict at the end of all the tests: I had experienced a cerebrovascular accident in the lower basal ganglia (a stroke, for the uninitiated). After twenty thousand dollars of medical care and tests came the five dollar prescription: an aspirin a day for life, and I should be good for another fifty years or so. And don't forget the annual checkups. (Doctors like guaranteed repeat customers, just like the rest of us.)

Did I think about my work and my career during that time? Yes, to the extent that I summoned my secretary to my bedside to help me finalize a report that was due to go out while I was indisposed. Yes, to the extent that I tried, unsuccessfully, to persuade my neurologist to let me go on a business trip to Venezuela just a week after the stroke. Yes, in the sense that I was keen to get back to work as soon as possible, to prove to everyone that I was still capable of doing the job. (My boss's response: "We always thought there was something wrong in your head. Now we have clinical evidence.") But the overwhelming concerns that I felt did not relate to work and career. They related to my family members—how the outcome of my illness would affect them.

When I was a child, it never occurred to me that life had a limited duration. As a teenager, I knew that people died, but assumed that I was exempt. That viewpoint persisted through my twenties. It was a shock, in my midthirties, to realize that I was not immortal, and the experience forced me to re-assess my priorities.

In 1984, after Senator Paul Tsongas of Massachusetts had been diagnosed with a form of lymphatic cancer and announced that he would not seek re-election, a friend wrote to him, "Nobody on his deathbed ever said 'I wish I had spent more time on my business.'" That may be true, but Cecil Rhodes's reported last words, "So little done, so much to do," seem to come very close. Rhodes (1853–1902) is best known today in America for the scholarships that he endowed and that still bear his name. In his own lifetime, though, he was noted as a great architect and advocate of British imperialism. He served as prime minister of the Cape, and he used his great personal wealth to expand his imperialist dream. This included attempting to annex several territories, and bringing the Rhodesias under British dominion. Most biographers assume that his last words lament his failure to complete the dream of British expansion. Or was he, perhaps, bewailing the fact that his life had been so driven by ambition that he had missed out on human warmth and closeness? Was that the "much" that he had failed to accomplish?

Nothing lasts forever in this life. Southern Rhodesia is now Zimbabwe, and Northern Rhodesia is Zambia. History books record the deeds of famous men, but in time their monuments crumble.

Should we, then, simply cry out "vanity of vanities," and not bother trying to achieve anything? Of course not. We humans have an insatiable need to be doing, creating something. This is Maslow's Level 5, which I personally believe is a mark left on our lives by a creative God. Whether or not you accept this explanation, it is plain that this need, this drive, is present within us and all around us. If we don't direct it into positive, constructive objectives, then we must channel it into negative, destructive ones. Every aspect of society displays the results of this, whether it is the effort invested in bringing a major construction project into being, developing a career, or building a family—or dealing drugs. We must create, but we must invest wisely in our creations.

Our careers are among the most important of our creations, and they require a great deal of time and effort to build and maintain. In my own case, when my stroke occurred, I had worked hard for more than twelve years since leaving university to develop my skills as a process engineer and later as a manager, and those twelve years were built on seventeen earlier years of formal academic study.

As with most people, a large part of my self-esteem comes from my work. I delight in the challenges of new projects, opportunities to meet new people in different parts of the world, the thrill of making a sale, and the sense of accomplishment when a job is successfully completed. I hope, when it is all over, people will look back on my contribution approvingly. A career is a treasure, not to be discarded lightly.

Yet in the final analysis a career is not all-important. The question I have had to ask myself repeatedly is this: What is the most important legacy that I will leave behind? The answer that I cannot avoid is that it is the impact I have on the people that I interact with, and especially my family, and not any work project or professional accomplishment. Jobs and even careers change easily, but a commitment "till death us do part" is profound and wonderful. That commitment is challenged every day within the realities of living, but it is binding and must not be taken lightly.

Moreover the most profound creative processes are not those that build skyscrapers or factories. Rather, they are the ones that shape people. Within my working environment as an engineer, the most important legacy is not the process designs I have created or improved; it is the people I have mentored and helped forward in their own careers. But more important still is my role in guiding my children to maturity, shaping their values, helping them find their way in life.

The challenge is to find the right balance: recognizing priorities, and applying ourselves to deal with them appropriately. I wish I could honestly say that I have the right balance. In truth I am still struggling with this issue, and I see many of my colleagues in the same dilemma. Yet perhaps it is an important first step simply to realize that it is all right to have family as a priority, despite the constant pressure to push for professional advancement at all costs. If this sometimes results in lost professional opportunities, so be it.

I would rather be considered uncommitted in my work than to have my children ask me in twenty years' time, "Where were you while I was growing up, Daddy?"

"As for man, his days are like the grass, he flourishes like a flower of the field; the wind blows over it, and its place remembers it no more" (Psalm 103:15–16).

Appendix

Text of the Hippocratic Oath

I swear by Apollo the physician, and Aesculapius, and Health, and All-heal, and all the gods and goddesses, that, according to my ability and judgment, I will keep this Oath and this stipulation to reckon him who taught me this Art equally dear to me as my parents, to share my substance with him, and relieve his necessities if required; to look upon his offspring in the same footing as my own brothers, and to teach them this art, if they shall wish to learn it, without fee or stipulation; and that by precept, lecture, and every other mode of instruction, I will impart a knowledge of the Art to my own sons, and those of my teachers, and to disciples bound by a stipulation and oath according to the law of medicine, but to none others. I will follow that system of regimen which, according to my ability and judgment, I consider for the benefit of my patients, and abstain from whatever is deleterious and mischievous. I will give no deadly medicine to any one if asked, nor suggest any such counsel; and in like manner I will not give to a woman a pessary to produce abortion. With purity and with holiness I will pass my life and practice my Art. I will not cut persons laboring under the stone, but will leave this to

Professional Excellence: Beyond Technical Competence, by Alan Rossiter
Copyright © 2008 John Wiley & Sons, Inc.

be done by men who are practitioners of this work. Into whatever houses I enter, I will go into them for the benefit of the sick, and will abstain from every voluntary act of mischief and corruption; and, further from the seduction of females or males, of freemen and slaves. Whatever, in connection with my professional practice or not, in connection with it, I see or hear, in the life of men, which ought not to be spoken of abroad, I will not divulge, as reckoning that all such should be kept secret. While I continue to keep this Oath unviolated, may it be granted to me to enjoy life and the practice of the art, respected by all men, in all times! But should I trespass and violate this Oath, may the reverse be my lot!

References

1. Abraham H. Maslow. *Motivation and Personality*, 3rd ed. Longman, New York, 1987.

2. Frank G. Goble. *The Third Force: The Psychology of Abraham Maslow*. Grossman, New York, 1970.

3. Steven M. Cahn, ed. *Classics of Western Philosophy*, 2nd ed. Hackett, Indianapolis, 1985, p. 114.

4. "Satisfaction Guaranteed." *The Chemical Engineer*, November 11, 1993, pp. 22–25.

5. Jyoti Thottam. "Thank God It's Monday." *Time*, January 17, 2005.

6. Amy Stevens. "Why Lawyers Are Depressed, Anxious, Bored Insomniacs." *Wall Street Journal*, June 12, 1995.

7. Sue Shellenbarger. "In Real Life, Hard Choices Upset Any Balancing Act," *Wall Street Journal*, April 19, 1995.

8. Hal Lancaster. "Engineering Is Re-Engineered into a Team Sport," *Wall Street Journal*, May 2, 1995.

9. Patrick Hanks, ed. *Hamlin Encyclopedic World Dictionary*, Hamlin, London, 1971.

10. Jim McIngvale with Dave White. *Elvis Is on the Lot*. Swan Publishing, Alvin, TX, 1996, p. 82.

11. *The Merriam-Webster Dictionary*. Pocket Books, New York, 1974.

12. "Ethics." Microsoft® Encarta® Online Encyclopedia, 2004, http://encarta.msn.com ©1997–2004 Microsoft Corporation. All Rights Reserved. Accessed June 21, 2004.

13. National Society of Professional Engineers (NSPE). "The Engineers' Creed," http://www.nspe.org/ethics/eh1-cred.asp. Accessed October 5, 2007.

14. National Society of Professional Engineers (NSPE). "Code of Ethics for Engineers," http://www.nspe.org/ethics/eh1-code.asp. Accessed December 26, 2006.

15. V. R. Manoj. "Hippocrates and Bioethics," http://www.vrmanoj.com/hippo.html. Accessed December 26, 2006.

16. Stephen R Covey. *The Seven Habits of Highly Effective People*. Simon and Schuster, London, 1992, p. 235.

17. Maryann V. Piotrowski. *Better Business Writing*. Piatkus, Ltd., London, 1991.

18. J. M. Morse, ed. *Webster's Standard American Style Manual*. Merriam-Webster, Springfield, MA, 1985.

19. *Communication Skills for Engineers and Scientists*. Institution of Chemical Engineers, Rugby, England, 1994.

20. Karen Beck. *Communicating at Work*. Seminar, Rossiter and Associates, Bellaire, TX, 2005.

21. John C. Maxwell. *Developing the Leader within You*. Thomas Nelson, Nashville, 1993, p. 23.

22. Stephen R Covey, op. cit., p. 151.

23. Texas Engineering Practice Act and Board Rules. "Professional Conduct and Ethics," §137.59, http://www.tbpe.state.tx.us/downloads/law_rules1206.pdf. Accessed December 26, 2006.

24. Ibid. §1001.302.

25. Robert Fulgum. *All I Really Need to Know I Learned in Kindergarten*. Villard, New York, 1990, p. 6.

26. The Merriam-Webster Dictionary. Pocket Books, New York, 1974.

27. Karen Beck, op. cit.
28. Doug Hissong. "Work More Effectively with Others." *Chemical Engineering Progress*, February 2004, pp. 55–58.
29. Douglas McGregor. "The Human Side of Enterprise", McGraw-Hill, 1960.
30. Team in Training, http://www.teamintraining.org/. Accessed December 30, 2006.
31. Rodney Atkins. *Watching You.* On the album *If You're Going Through Hell*, ASIN: B000FS9MYC, Curb Records, 2006.
32. Partick Morley. *The Man in the Mirror.* Zondervan, Grand Rapids, 1997, p. 122.
33. Dan Bolin and Ken Sutterfield. *How to Be Your Little Man's Dad: 365 Things to Do with Your Son.* Piñon Press, Colorado Springs, 1993.
34. Leonard Cohen. *Anthem.* On the album *The Future.* ASIN: B0000028W9, Sony, 1992.

Index